THE WOMAN IN THE MOUNTAIN

THE WOMAN IN THE MOUNTAIN

RECONSTRUCTIONS OF SELF AND LAND BY ADIRONDACK WOMEN WRITERS

KATE H. WINTER

State University of New York Press

Published by
State University of New York Press, Albany

©1989 State University of New York

For information, address State University of New York
Press, State University Plaza, Albany, N.Y., 12246

Library of Congress Cataloging-in-Publication Data

Winter, Kate H.
    The Woman in the mountain : reconstructions of self and land by
Adirondack women writers / Kate H. Winter.
        p.   c.m
    Bibliography: p.
    ISBN 0-88706-886-3.   ISBN 0-88706-888-X (pbk.)
    1. American literature--New York (State)--Adirondack Mountains-
-History and criticism.   2. American literature--New York (State)-
-Adirondack Mountains.   3. American literature--Women authors-
-History and criticism.   4. American literature--Women authors.
5. Women and literature--New York (State)--Adirondack Mountains.
6. Adirondack Mountains (N.Y.) in literature.   7. Adirondack
Mountains (N.Y.)--Literary collections.   8. Mountain life in
literature.   9. Landscape in literature.   10. Self in literature.
11. Women--New York (State)--Adirondack Mountains--Intellectual
life. I. Title.
PS253.N7W56 1989
810'.9'3274753--dc19   88-6960
                                                          CIP

For my mother,
Margaret Everett Hughs,
who understands about challenges

Contents

Acknowledgments

The photographs of these authors were generously made available by: Noel Riedinger-Johnson (Jeanne Robert Foster and Lucia Newell Oliviere), Ken Lawless (Adelaide Crapsey), Anne LaBastille, Maitland DeSormo (Martha Reben), Alice Gilborn (photo by Craig Gilborn), and Jean Rikhoff (photo by Judith Madison).

This work was furthered by a faculty research grant from the State University of New York at Albany. Additional support and encouragement came from the many Adirondackers who spent their time and lent their materials, especially Noel Riedinger-Johnson, Maitland DeSormo, the people at the Adirondack Museum, and the friends and heirs of the women I write of here.

The following publishers have also contributed to this volume by their permission to reprint. For Jeanne Robert Foster materials, my thanks to Syracuse University Press and for Alice Gilborn's "Portents" to The Greenfield Review Press. "Among My Closest Friends" is from *Woodswoman* by Anne LaBastille, copyright 1976 by Anne LaBastille, reprinted by permission of E. P. Dutton, a division of NAL Penguin, Inc. "A Copycat Walden" and "Sauntering Around Lilypad Lake" are reprinted from *Beyond Black Bear Lake* by Anne LaBastille, by permission of W. W. Norton and Company, Inc. Copyright 1987 by Anne LaBastille. The Reben selections from *A Sharing of Joy*, copyright 1963 by Martha Reben, are reprinted by permission of Harcourt Brace Jovanovich, Inc.

Special thanks are due to Linda Hazard Hughs and Meg Hess Seckendorf for their help with the book and to my son Jeffrey and my husband Gene for their boundless love and patience.

Introduction

Over the last one hundred fifty years, the Adirondack mountain region has been described, dissected and mythologized by writers as diverse as Ralph Waldo Emerson and Joyce Carol Oates. It has been recreated so often by literary and scientific imaginations that by the 1880s more had been written about the Adirondack country than any other wilderness area in the United States.[1] Philip Terrie's book on the Adirondacks and environmental aesthetics reveals that the nineteenth century view of the mountains was essentially a masculine one.[2] A survey of Jamieson's *Adirondack Reader* confirms that.[3] Although the editor has been meticulous about including women's texts, there seem to be few. With that realization, I began my search for women's renderings of the Adirondack experience.

The subject under study was how the female imagination responded to the mountain environment. There are many women whose works might be included in this collection, and most of them are listed in the bibliography at the end of this volume. My goal, however, was to scrutinize the *literary* responses of women writers, the ways in which they imaginatively recreated their lives and the landscape. Therefore, the words included in my study are limited to fiction, poetry and autobiography, which I define as at least a partially fictive genre. I have omitted writing which was merely about the mountains — trail guides, histories, biographies of mountain characters.

Furthermore, a work such as Dorothy W. Goodfellow's *Growing Up Wild*, which details the author's young years near Silver Bay, is missing from these pages because of its fierce clinging to literal facts about life at the edge of the wilderness in the early twentieth century. It lacks an imaginative connection with the landscape, as do the diaries of Adirondack women that I read. Spanning the years 1854–1937, the Blue Mountain Lake collection is full of the detail of daily, domestic concerns with almost no commentary. The landscape itself plays almost no part in their rendering of their lives. What little introspection or probing that appears is limited to vague, lingering unease. Even the death of a child or husband is simply recounted as another hazard of living told without the nuance of emotional response. These personal pieces are oddly impersonal, as though written to record and validate the incidents in a difficult life. They are ledgers of paltry transactions, chillingly austere and remote.

In my search for women's expressions of the imaginative landscape, I further limited my study to writers who had actually lived a substantial or significant part of their lives in the Adirondack region, an area which more or less conformed to the boundaries established by the blue line, the cartographer's mark that defined the Adirondacks. Some interesting works can only be listed here because there was not enough biographical information available to determine whether the author was an Adirondack woman or not. Typically, the lives of lesser known women writers were obscured by silence and neglect. Therefore, Francine Findley's novel *From What Dark Roots*, a very readable story of the struggle for utopian ideals amidst the mountain reality of the land near Malone, can only be mentioned. Dorothy Palmer Hines' fictional account of the lives and loves of tuberculosis patients in Saranac Lake, *No Wind of Healing*, is recommended but not included. My selection was further reduced by my eliminating writers who, like many of the male writers, only visited the mountains and used them for imaginative fodder and picturesque settings. Even as fine a work as Joyce Carol Oates's *Bellefleur*, an Adirondack gothic novel, is not discussed here because its author did not live and work in the mountains. For the seven women whose lives and works *are* collected, the mountain landscape is both geographic and symbolic.

The choice among pieces to be included was shaped by my sense that readers with little background coming upon these writers would need works that were quickly accessible and said something directly to the reader about the experience of living in the Adirondack environment. In addition, I chose samples which I found to be the best and most representative writing of each author. One may read through the selections as they are ordered here and find a kind of lyric dance, a balance of poetry and prose in which each piece seems to move naturally from the flow of the previous works. They are organically connected; the resonances grow.

The ordering violates linear chronology from the beginning with the poetry of Jeanne Robert Foster's mother appearing *after* her daughter's. The reader will, I think, find more power in Oliviere's poems after dipping into the daughter's and thus will see the tension in the mother/daughter relation, a connection more clearly seen in retrospect. Elaine Showalter's notion that "a woman's text is not only mothered but parented," that it has both maternal and paternal precursors and stretches the inheritances from both, has also informed the arrangement.[4] Crapsey's style coming crisply after the first two poets' work is a sudden divergence into new forms which in turn anticipate the prose of Anne LaBastille. The proximity of LaBastille's and Reben's prose kindles our consciousness of literary influence and links them both in the tradition of male and female autobiography thereby touching the poetry and prose of Gilborn which follows. Rikhoff, the only novelist in the group, mingles all of the elements of the preceding narratives, poetry and autobiography, and so concludes the collection.

In Rikhoff's case, the piece from *Butte's Landing* was chosen because it can stand apart from the rest of the novel without tottering, and it exemplifies the issues of identity and quest with which all of Rikhoff's novels struggle.

The Adirondacks were a unique kind of frontier compared to the others which Americans earlier had pushed open. Distinguished by the variety of terrain it offered—swamp and bog, lake and shore, deciduous and evergreen forests, the timberline and finally the alpine peaks—the region had largely been bypassed during the westward movement of the population after the Revolutionary War because of its inaccessibility and the seeming worthlessness of untillable land. In winter it was too rugged even for the Iroquois, so there was little threat from Indians who only used it to hunt and fish in season. When the wooded vastness was opened around the turn of the nineteenth century, it quickly became a significant literary and industrial symbol for American writers, thinkers, businessmen and sportsmen.

Before the Civil War, women rarely ventured into the mountains for recreation.[5] What women were to be found there were part of settlers' families or independent businesswomen trading on the lumber and guide enterprises.

Most of the men who travelled in the mountains for business or sport enjoyed the pleasures of the outdoors, but "they often felt psychologically disoriented in the wilderness, and they were overtly hostile to the idea of land that contributed nothing of commercial or agricultural value."[6] Some of the more enlightened travellers saw that there was great potential for wealth from the land and its minerals as well as for spiritual rejuvenation.[7] The latter notion, closely linked to the romantic idea of the healing powers of nature, percolated in the consciousness of some men to emerge in the later development of the Adirondacks as a health center. Within a few years of Murray's publication of *Adventures in the Wilderness* in 1869, the Adirondacks became the resort, and often the last resort, for tuberculosis patients. "Adirondack Murray," a Boston cleric and flamboyant outdoorsman, recounted the almost miraculous cure of a consumptive by the fresh mountain air laden with the scent of pine and balsam. Thus the idea of modern medicine was linked with the romantic idea of spiritual and mental healing which wood and pond could provide.

For the most part, however, men sought to exploit the land, and their imagery confirms the idea that earth—conceived as female—was theirs to subdue and use. In comparing women's texts to men's we risk falling back into the habit of looking at men's writing as the norm and women's as somehow deviant. It is more useful to celebrate these women's voices than to reduce them to such categorization. I suspect, as Elaine Showalter suggests, that women's writing is subtly and elusively different from men's in ways not readily described, defined and differentiated by talk about genre, style, biography, absence, content or any single model of difference.[8] Our reference point must always be the writing itself. My goal is to recover for us these voices from the Adirondack wilderness so that we can attend to the nuances of difference and the joy of the speaking. For most of the nineteenth century, they were silent.

The region was clearly perceived as a man's domain. As Emerson noted in the poem celebrating his camping trip in the mountains in 1858, men could, with considerable help from their guides, cast off the responsibilities of manhood and become like boys again. It is worth noting that his blissful transformation required all the paraphernalia of a major expedition, and the guides lifted the literal as well as figurative burdens of many responsibilities from these mountain ramblers.

Ironically, it seems that men feared the wilderness and its effects. Though liberated by the outdoors, they felt threatened by the possibility that man's reason, what separated him from animals, might desert him and that he might thus revert to being entirely uncivilized. In the wilderness, the possibility of moral and/or mental degeneration lurked behind the promise of freedom from cultural constraints. That view of wilderness is a portion of our Puritan inheritance in which the wild represents the darker, ungoverned side of human nature. Such a view, especially of mountainous wilderness, is not surprising when one considers the scriptural duality of mountain symbolism. In the Old Testament, hills and mountains did not have the terrible associations that we find in the New Testament. In Hebraic literature and art, hills are sacred places marked out for meditation, purification and apotheosis. In Christian scripture, there is a reversal which is emblematic of the social revolution embedded in the Christian tradition: "whether in external Nature or in the social scene, what was 'high' was suspect; what was 'low', more worthy."[9]

A milder Puritanism saw wilderness as a place to test oneself, to build character. These women writers also see wilderness as a testing ground, but as a place to *reveal* rather than create character. Wilderness is empowering, helping women to uncover and recover their latent talents and strengths. The basis of this curious disparity seems to lie in men's perceiving the wilderness as "the other." Carol Gilligan's study of the formation of identity and voice supports with developmental theory the dichotomy inherent in male and female approaches to the natural environment. If male development is based in a narrative of separation and failed relationships, especially with women, which teaches them an ethic of distance, separateness and loss, we can see the consequences in their responses to the land. It becomes both a place to recapture the camaraderie and integration with the female which signalled childhood and at the same time a place where the adult need to pursue, subdue and separate is culturally sanctioned. Furthermore, men fear what they cannot control, what is seen as separate from themselves and ungovernable. In their attempts to control that "other," they do things to it, not for or with it, for expedience: dominion becomes domination. On the other hand, women's development, based on continuing connection with the primary parent, turns inward toward an expansion of the sense of self and a recognition that the self requires and deserves nurture. Girls value relationships and caring over separation and remain connected to their environment. For women, this impulse to connectedness appears in "the moral imperative that emerges as an injunction to care, a responsibility to discern and alleviate the 'real and recognizable trouble' of this world."[10] Gilligan concludes that for women, truth lies in "connection, in the realization that self and other are interdependent and that life, however valuable in itself, can only be sustained by care in relationships."[11] These Adirondack women have expanded that understanding of responsibility by creating a larger web of care to include the earth.

Over-arching Gilligan's account is the fact of women's socialization. Women have been taught since Eve that wildness, irrationality, and reproduction are essential components of their beings. Thus they see nature in its wild state as part of themselves. One common strand which runs throughout the texts of these women writers is that their own sense of well-being is intimately connected to the well-being of the land. This is a position which discomfits some feminists because of what they see as a reversion to the roles of caretaker and nurturer that they have been straining against. The writers here show us a way to integrate—as Thoreau did—the need for autonomy and power with the nurturing function. All have given themselves physically as well as intellectually to the mountains and found therein a feeling of unity with rather than separation from the land, seeing themselves as creatures which are woven into the knot of life on this planet, beings who are in touch with a life force. Connected to this awareness of vitality is a reverence for all life. Out of that comes a certain antagonism toward hunters—anyone who preys on wilderness inhabitants, including the military—thus confirming Elaine and William Hedges' finding that among American women writers, there is a general uneasiness with hunters. That aversion contrasts startlingly with many male writers' characterization of hunters as the epitome of freedom, courage, self-sufficiency, and industry— the American virtues.[12] In one striking departure from this pattern, Paula Brandreth's *Trails of Enchantment*, which she published using the pseudonym "Paul," bespeaks a consciousness either not wholly feminine or consciously masculine in its glorification of hunting and fishing in the Adirondacks.

Unlike Brandreth, the other women studied for this volume resist the
impulse to intrude on nature, to meddle with her processes and tinker with
her systems. They are instead intent on preserving the virgin land—or re-
storing it—, the land with which they identify their whole selves. Similarly,
each writer is concerned in some measure with reclaiming her self from what
had been socialized away, recovering some of who she was before she was
taught what was acceptable and feminine.

Even writers and thinkers from outside could see the potential for self-
realization which the Adirondacks offered women. Kate Field, an international journalist, described her own visit to the Adirondacks during the
1860s in an essay "The Bloomer Girls." Field notes that the mountains are
thought of as a male domain because women, with their awful timidity,
recoil from the wild:

> They flaunt their muslins in the face of the backwoodsman and hover on
> the outskirts of the Wilderness, as if to say to their sex, "So far shalt thou go
> and no farther," while fathers, brothers, husbands, and sons grow away from
> them as they grow into sympathy with outdoor life. . . .Women made the
> town, and with all the ills to which she is heir and from which she will not
> emancipate herself. Even the beaver has its town house and country house,
> but wherever woman goes she carries brick walls and ballrooms with her.
> And she it is who is to mold the world anew![13]

After telling of her own trek in the mountains, she insists who it is who
ought to go into that wilderness: "women, because they are in the greatest
need of just such a life."[14] The outdoors could transform them, a meta-
morphosis shuddered at by the genteel tradition. Yet Field envisions a new
breed of American woman who is

> willing to be tanned, freckled, and even made to resemble antique statuary
> with well-developed limbs for the sake of renewed youth. Let such try the
> wilderness. "Life consists in wildness." "The most alive is the wildest.
> Dulness (*sic*) is but another name for tameness." Do you not believe me?
> Ask Thoreau.[15]

That is almost precisely what women did. Thoreau, embodying the
urge for full engagement with his surroundings and the search for an
elemental self, became a touchstone to the women writers represented here.
One is struck by how often they refer to Thoreau's *Walden*, either allusively
or directly. This seems especially ironic since Thoreau himself found mountains horrifying, especially Mt. Katahdin in Maine which he described in the
dread-filled image ". . . out of Chaos and Old Night."[16] However awed he may
have been by hills, his work combines several features which appealed

especially to these mountain writers. He joins the scientific precision of the naturalist with the intuition of the transcendentalist, thus blending what have been traditionally thought of as the male attributes of dissection and analysis with the female impulse toward integration and cohesion. Furthermore, Thoreau dramatically contradicts the primary hero of American literature who is typically a man in motion, moving through wilderness both real and figurative. Thoreau is rooted. Unlike most male writers and protagonists, he was not on his way somewhere. He created an image of the human being living in concord with the very nature with which women identified. He was concerned in *Walden* with domestic arrangements. Like women, he was preoccupied with creating a home, an edifice that would at once protect and liberate the spirit, a dwelling-place for the soul. The creation of such a place parallels the creation of a new self while the harmony of such a life comes in part from making a minimal change in the landscape, from adapting oneself rather than forcing adaptation on the wild. This intimacy with domestic arrangements touches women's lives, and the writers discussed here often use domestic imagery when speaking with women's voices as though to make more accessible to other women the mysteries of the wilderness.

I have been tempted not to discuss the physical beings of these women, in an effort to align myself with the tradition of scholarship which would insist that to be taken seriously we must have intellects but not bodies. These women are not disembodied consciousnesses. Their connections with the land, weather, work and love are important elements in their responses to the mountains. They truly lived in the Adirondacks—and even died in them—viscerally, elementally. For that reason, I have tried to tell the stories of their lives as well as of their works. We would do well to model our inquiry on the Chinese character for Thought which is the combination of the calligraphy characters for Heart and Brain.[17] In thinking about these women and their works, and in my presentation of them, I have tried to be faithful to that image, just as the writers themselves melded heart and brain in their recreation of the landscape.

For Jeanne Robert Foster, Crane Mountain near Johnsburg was connected in some mysterious way to the poet's consciousness of herself. When she was a girl she found a place on Crane where the mountain rose straight up like a wall. She would secretly go there and lean against the mountain with outstretched arms, embracing it until "there seemed to be a strong force passing through me, so untamed and wild and beautiful that there are no words for it." Foster believed that her birth and identity were linked to the mountain and that when she died she would remain "alive in the intelligence that moves in Crane." The difficulty of a hardscrapple life on an Adirondack farm forced Jeanne to live with various relatives, an uprooting that took her into the lives and homes of diverse characters. Against the rough realities of such a life, the young poet forged a self both independent and adventure-some yet fiercely connected to the values and people of the North Country. Her travels abroad, her career in journalism, her passion for art—nothing supplanted her love of the mountains and its folk. In her poetry we see again rough-hewn characters fighting to live a meaningful life. Her mother, Lucia Newell Oliviere, had also been an Adirondacker and a poet. Born just before the Civil War, she was the daughter of a lumberman who drowned on a log drive. That adversity required that she also be "farmed out," but eventually she was educated at Albany Normal School and became a teacher. Her poems, like her daughter's, distill an era and character that have essentially vanished from the woods.

Adelaide Crapsey, on the other hand, was not born to the mountains. Her early life in Rochester, New York, as one of eleven children of an Episcopal clergyman's family, shaped her to be a distinguished scholar and teacher. Her travel abroad charged her talent with energy even as her health failed dismally. At the age of thirty-four she was stricken with the unmis-takable signs of tuberculosis and went to Saranac Lake to cure. It was there that her two finest contributions to American poetry—her best verses and the cinquain form—were produced. The death she saw represented in the graveyard just beyond her window, her tendency for repression and com-pression, and the bleakness of those seasons spent in the region's grip with its aura of illness and despair combined to wrench from her the poetic achievement of her last year.

Anne LaBastille stumbled into the Adirondacks looking for work and there discovered the woman she had always wanted to be—a woodswoman. Born in New York City and raised in suburban New Jersey, she took a job at an Adirondack hotel, and her interest in wildlife began to grow from a vague passion to what is now a centered, fiercely protective love. Adirondack guide, international wildlife consultant, and writer, she has chronicled the emergence of a self that lives in accord with the forces of the wilderness. LaBastille's work recreates the daily struggle of living a meaningful life.

Martha Reben, battling tuberculosis and struggling to breathe, took to the woods to write a similar story. She went to the Adirondacks seeking a cure for her illness and found herself. A child of New York City, Reben took refuge in the woods at Weller Pond when conventional cures for TB proved too painful and futile. Her books remain as testament not only to the remarkable healing power of the wilderness but to the emerging spirit of in-dependence and self-reliance which living in the wild gave to Reben.

Like LaBastille and Reben, Alice Wolf Gilborn came from beyond the blue line. Raised on the outskirts of Denver, she was sent East to college at Wellesley. While there she often found it too expensive to return to Col-orado for vacations, so she visited at Au Sable Forks with a friend and came to think of the Adirondacks as her second home. Settled since 1972 in Blue Mountain Lake, Gilborn is probably best known for her work as editor of *Blueline*. Her editorial essays and her articles in *Adirondack Life* reveal her concern with the creative life of mountain artists—sculptors, writers, painters, poets. In her prose and poetry we find the recurring idea of living against the land, creating a life that is authentic, satisfying and survivable in an environment that constantly forces one to confront her own vulnerable humanity.

Jean Rikhoff's characters similarly confront the essential facts of their being. In her trilogy of North Country novels, her command of North Country character and narrative belies a consciousness that is intimately connected to the people and land of the Adirondack region but is in no way parochial. Rikhoff, like most of these writers, came to the mountains as a young woman. She was raised in Indianapolis and educated in the east where she went to escape the flatness of midwestern thinking. Immediately after graduate school, she lit out for the territory—Europe—to write and teach. Eventually she chose to move to the Adirondack region to teach, live and write as well as edit *The Glens Falls Review*. Rikhoff is convinced that geography is crucial to character, and her characters affirm themselves by enduring against the trials of weather and mountains.

It is reductive to classify these women, so I have endeavored to explore the ways in which they are similar. To begin with, most had particularly strong mothers, often women who were also writers. Many also had problematic relationships with their fathers, men who were either terribly close or painfully distant. This could be said of many writers, but the signal difference here is the degree to which the parental relationships—or failure of them—pushed the women to find their own limits and identities. Perhaps as part of that search, most of these women either renounced or by curious circumstances were denied the security of husbands and lovers, and lived instead as single, self-supporting women. They are similarly independent and free-thinking in spiritual matters. Most of them cast away early definitions of faith and denomination to embrace some combination of spiritual practice—deism, pantheism, mysticism, spiritualism—which freed and yet nurtured them. Their writing is brimming with religious imagery, visions of paradise, and new deities that live among all creatures. With heart and head these writers recreate a world in which women and men are committed to claiming the self in unity with creation. They have found the woman in the mountain.

Jeanne Robert Foster

Jeanne Robert Foster

Crane Mountain near Johnsburg was connected in some mysterious way to the poet Jeanne Foster's consciousness of herself. When she was a girl she found a place on Crane Mountain where it rose straight up like a wall. She would secretly go there and lean against the mountainside, embracing it with arms outstretched until "There seemed to be a strong force passing through me, so untamed wild and beautiful that there are no words for it."[1] As a child Foster learned to share her mountain with others: she guided tourists on hikes up Crane Mountain for twenty-five cents per party. Two of the poems included here, "Shadbush" and "Shadders," are about that mountain. As Foster remembered it, during the time that her mother was pregnant with her, she stayed at home looking at Crane Mountain which loomed in front of the house. Jeanne believed that her birth and identity were linked to the mountain and that when she died she would remain "very much alive in the intelligence that moves in Crane."[2] The girl barely survived her birth in 1879. The doctor, believing the infant had died during delivery, put her aside on the windowsill and turned his attention to the mother. An hour later he realized that the child still lived. It was a beginning that signalled the tenacity and passion for living that always characterized Foster and her work.

Her mother was a school teacher, Lizzy (Lucia) Oliver, whose own poetry is included in this collection. Lizzy, who had lived and taught outside the region, urged her daughter to seek life in a world wider than the mountains. Her father, Frank Oliver, a lumberjack, was a "soft-spoken, deeply religious man"[3] with an intense love of the land and its people. The difficulty of scratching out a living for the family required that the girl be "farmed out" to various relatives including the Francis Putnams of the same family that had taken in her own mother years before. That may seem to be a wrenching hardship for a child. Perhaps, however, being passed between families and travelling among the mountain villages and folk with her uncle who was a peddler afforded the impressionable girl a wider-ranging view of the mountains and their people. No doubt such early independence from her family gave her the confidence to strike out on her own and to overcome whatever handicaps afflicted her, including a slight speech defect and one damaged heart valve from rheumatic fever which she had when she was fourteen. In spite of her childhood difficulties, she endured. Surviving in the harsh environment was not an end in itself, however. Foster wanted much more.

From early in her life she was looking for an identity, trying to create a self in keeping with her mother's and her own sense of herself as a gifted, vigorous and beautiful woman. Her use of pseudonyms is suggestive. Some she took from male family names: "Jean" from an ancestor who died fighting the Indians and "Robert" from another French forebear. Her ethnic identity and subsequent passion for Irish letters was inherited from her grandfather who was "black Irish" and about whom she wrote: ". . . all I have ever done I owe to his blood."[4] As much as she may have identified with her male ancestors, she was committed to her feminine self. When she was fifteen she followed her mother's career and became a teacher, being certified to teach third grade in Warren County for which she received $5.00 a week. She boarded with district families but returned home on weekends to work in the woods with her father. The following year she was certified to teach second grade. Within another year she had resigned to marry an insurance man and move away from her beloved mountains to Rochester, New York. Her husband, Matlock Foster, a man older than her father, recognized her potential and determined to help her develop it. He enabled Jeanne to graduate from the Rochester Athenaem and Mechanics Institute and later took her to New York City where her opportunities expanded dramatically.

Jeanne Foster was a great beauty, a fact which she enjoyed and a gift she shared. Her bronze hair capped a form and face that, even to late twentieth century eyes, is enticing in its regularity and charm. From working in fashion journalism, she became a model, appearing on the cover of *Vanity Fair* and posing for some of the most important illustrators of the time, including Charles Dana Gibson and Harrison Fisher, becoming the famous "Fisher Girl." She delighted in her physicality and sensuality, even declaring in her journal that physical passion is the equivalent of religious fervor. Her letters, diaries, and poems celebrate what is sensual, even erotic, in art, fashion, landscape, and human relationships. She was a woman who lived passionately through her friendships, her loves, and her work, whatever it was at the moment.

Foster's writing began early: when she was eight, she was writing detailed letters to her parents about school and her life among the relatives she was living with. She worked at stories and poems and in 1898 published her first article in a Vermont journal. The years in New York exposed her to the galleries, museums, and literary life of the city which was second only to Paris for cosmopolitanism. Her modelling work was successful, though perhaps trivial, and she was beautiful enough for the stage, so she studied at the Stanhope-Wheatcroft Dramatic School and had several small roles with the American Stock Company. Experience on the stage suggested a new direction in her writing. An unpublished play *Black Forest* and her prize-winning play *Marthe* show her experimenting with genre and, as a trained actress, thinking about new audiences and ways to share her vision with them. Meanwhile she was writing short fiction and had published at least one short story in 1902. She and her husband moved to Boston so Jeanne could care for her sister; there, after winning a contests at the *Boston American*, she took a job writing reviews and features including some tough-minded exposés.[5]

The time in Boston gave her the opportunity to study through Harvard University courses while she got a firm grounding in journalism. At *The American Review of Reviews* she developed as a writer and thinker, doing book and poetry reviews, essays on art, education and the theater as well as stories she sent back as a war correspondent from Britain. When she returned to New York City, she was introduced into the literary circle centered at the Petitpas restaurant where John Butler Yeats, artist and father of poet William Butler Yeats, held court. Her friendship with Yeats lasted until his death in 1922. She buried him in the Chestertown Rural Cemetery near the Foster family plot. Their friendship nurtured her interest in the Irish literary renaissance. It was also through Yeats that she met John Quinn, the art patron and man whom she was to love fiercely until his death. Quinn fostered her innate taste for the avant-garde and educated her in artistic matters. Ultimately he came to depend on her as he assembled the most significant collection of contemporary French art in America. She accompanied him often to Europe where she met

Yeats' son William, James Joyce, T. S. Eliot, Ezra Pound and Ford Madox Ford. Eventually she became American editor of the *transatlantic review*. After Quinn's death, she continued to write, although she spent much of her time caring for her ailing family until, within the following few years, most of them, including her husband, had died. She returned permanently to Schenectady and turned forever away from the bustling glamor of her life in New York. She spent most of her remaining years working for the public welfare as her mother before her had, particularly to improve the living conditions of the elderly in Schenectady.

In the early days the editor of *The American Review of Reviews* had invited Foster to work on a book on the Civil War. She selected pieces gleaned from her Adirondack neighbors for the section on poetry and songs of the war. It was the beginning of her use of specifically Adirondack material. While abroad working on articles for the *Review of Reviews*, she was already composing the poetry for *Neighbors of Yesterday* and *Wild Apples* which appeared in 1916, mingling her discovery of literary traditions with writing in her own North Country idiom. Her work in diverse modes including vernacular poetry continued intermittently, and in 1957 she was awarded first prize in both the Pennsylvania Poetry Society and the Tennessee Poetry Society competitions. In 1963, her book *Neighbors of Yesterday*, first published in 1916, was republished by friends in Schenectady. Encouraged by the reception of that volume, she renewed work on a collection of her Adirondack poems composed of true stories recreated in verse. She struggled to finish it but was overtaken by death in 1970 at age ninety-one. Recently the daughter of those same friends has uncovered the cache of poems, letters, prose pieces and photographs and published them at last as a final testament to the enduring love of the mountains and its people.

From her upcountry upbringing in a household dominated by protestant theology and a social gospel of reform, Foster's consciousness enlarged as she passed through her belief that "the universe has its source in a creator with an intelligent design, not only for man but for creations such as animals and plants"[6] to the eastern philosophy and belief in reincarnation that emerges in the posthumously published verses in *Awakening Grace*. By 1906 she was a member of the Theosophical Society, a group which advocated an eclectic, worldwide religion based on Brahmanic and Buddhistic teachings. Hers was a spiritual journey requiring enormous energy and freedom of thought, an intellectual habit instilled by her mother who herself believed in mysticism and spiritualism.

Her aesthetic was as wide-ranging and expansive as her thinking. Much of her work is free verse shaped by the cadences of the Old Testament and modified by the speech rhythms of the North Country. A believer in archetypal images in the unconscious which flow into poetry carrying with them their own musical laws, she turned in her later poems to the strikingly realistic, place-specific poetry which represents her best work. In all of the Adirondack poems she has attempted to recreate the rhythms and spirit of Adirondack speech. In contrast, the earliest poems, which appeared in 1916 in *Wild Apples*, are energetic and discursive, but the materials, forms, and diction are borrowed from the conventional poetry of the late nineteenth and early twentieth centuries. The result is verse which shows a poetic sensibility struggling to find its voice. She recognized the roughness resulting from the conflict and apologized for the "very crude and childish"[7] poems in that volume. In the same year her *Neighbors of Yesterday* appeared showing the poet at work in a very different mode. Because these mountain poems are so prosaic, one wonders why she chose poetic forms. In her own words, she did it "for the same reason . . . as did Alexander Pope—it was more economical."[8] Foster's prose-poems are most reminiscent of the work of Robert Frost whose poems are similarly rooted in his own landscape and are part of the revival of poetry that occurred in the early decades of this century. With little use of metaphor and simile, they rely on concrete, rural images rendered faithfully. To capture the feel of mountain speech, she often used the unaccented iambic line. The Adirondack poems, spare and flinty with none of the conventional sentimentality that marks the earlier poems, grapple with the gritty facts of life in the North Country. The characters are beset by poverty, isolation, madness, religious fervor, misspent love and death. Underlying all is a fierce stubbornness approaching mania. The songs and tales of the lumberjacks that appear in *Neighbors* and *Adirondack Portraits* are not merely entertaining nostalgia. They capture the sound and fury of raw life in the lumber camps, an achievement which—apart from its poetic worth—preserves a vanished era. Like the New England local colorists, Foster is more interested in the people who inhabit the region and how the landscape molds them as they pit themselves against it. There is little of the triumph that readers find in Rikhoff and LaBastille, or even the gentle coexistence that Reben described.

In 1977, seven years after Foster's death, a volume of poetry titled *Awakening Grace* was published, edited by the friends of Foster's in Schenectady who had first told her of the guru Meher Baba thirty years earlier. Jeanne subsequently met him twice and accepted him as the avatar. The collection of poems is composed of hymns, meditations, invocations, and songs rejoicing in spiritual love and celebrating the many manifestations of the god. Although driven by authentic spiritual belief, the pieces lack the polish that Foster's other work shows. Apparently the poet herself did not intend them as public poems but as private outpourings. They are primarily interesting for the insight they give into their creator's religious quest. Throughout her life, the prose—which she felt was most important because it did the most good in the world—and her experiments with conventional verse forms and drama are diversions from the passionate, rooted poems of her Adirondack days.

So the publication of her last work in Riedinger-Johnson's *Adirondack Portraits* represents the artist returning to the visceral, bone-jarring truths that she knew from her early life among mountain folk. In those poems she wrestles with the disparity between the man's and the woman's experience of the landscape and the human grandeur of the people who clung to the hillsides leading a hardscrabble life. One sees in these poems the gift for narrative and eye for telling detail that could have easily made her a fiction writer like Philander Deming or Sarah Orne Jewett. These are not celebrations of wilderness but of the people who struggled against it in a mythic effort to tame the mountains.

Hers was a journey that took her far from the upcountry that shaped her. However, the intimacy and sensitivity with which she explored and claimed the landscape as her own grounded her in the values that years of travel abroad (eight trips in all) and the glitter of cosmopolitan life could not supplant. One is tempted to tell Foster's story by listing the well-known writers, artists, editors—the great men—with whom she was connected, but to do so focuses a reader's attention on peripheral matters. All that is really needed to validate Jeanne Robert Foster as a poet is what she left, her testament to the enduring values of the Adirondack people.

WHAT YOU SHALL SAY

Do not say of me: She was
Beautiful or kind or good.
Say: There was an April song
Once—she heard and understood.

PETITION

Yea of Thy Mercy Lord this greatest boon;
I who have drunk Thy largess fair and free
Sue that Thou save me from Time's misery
That lays foul hands on beauty late or soon.
Before chill years my burning heart shall swoon,
Translate untouched to immortality
My lovely gauds—I pray Thee piteously,
Who guarded them until my ripened noon!

Yea—let me come into Thy presence, Lord,
Sweet-fashioned, lithe of limb, with breasts adored;
Firm muscled waist, strong shining, milk-white thighs,
Lips like sweet foliage and soft-coloured eyes.
Yea of Thy pity, Lord, save from Time's lust
Thy handiwork; hell is to turn to dust.

INTO DIMNESS

I heard the wild loon and the catbird cry
Over Sagamore Lake, and knew that I

Heard the ancient call of race
Bidding me to my own place.

> I am the root of the yellow willow,
> The stem of the lily leaf;
> There cannot come to my marsh-grass pillow
> The cry of a human grief.

I heard the bluejay scream and the squirrel chitter
On the edge of the wood, and felt the bitter
Cold of the mist upon my face
Bidding me to my own place.

> I am the root of the yellow willow,
> The stem of the lily leaf;
> There cannot come to my marsh-grass pillow
> The cry of a human grief.

JEN MURDOCK'S ROOSTERS

Nature don't listen to us very much.
When we tell her what to do, she veers off
On some road she had in her mind
Before we were born. Smart men tell us now
That they're digging down into her secrets,
But when they've dug out just how she does things
And set it all down, she'll pull out a trick
That's brand new.

                    When I think about it all—
I remember Jen Murdock's hens; their eggs
Seemed to hatch mostly roosters, not pullets.
They were just barnyard fowls; you couldn't tell
What breed they were; they had mixed-up feathers,
But when one of them "set" and Jen gave her nest eggs
Expecting to raise some laying pullets,
Like as not she'd get a brood of roosters.

One day last spring Jen came down to my place
And said, "I want to borrow a setting of eggs;
There's something queer about my hens.
When their eggs hatch, the chicks are all roosters.
I've heard that round eggs will hatch out pullets.
So pick out thirteen round eggs—no long ones."
I brought out the egg crock and Jen picked up
A setting of *round* eggs.

       She was lucky:
They all hatched; she had thirteen fine chickens.
Her husband, Rob, built a new coop for them.
They grew fast, and when they were feathered out
Rob would listen at the coop now and then
And call: "Jen, you've got another rooster."
It went on until—there was no mistake—
Jen had twelve roosters out of round eggs.
One chick looked like a pullet; the next week
When Rob came into the house after milking,
"Guess what, Jen," he said. *"Your pullet's crowing."*

THE WILDERNESS IS STRONG

Here in the wilderness folks will tell you
To be careful about the place you live,
For there's something in the mountains
And the hills that is stronger than people,
And you will grow like the place where you live.
The hands of the mountains reach out
With bindings that hold the heart forever.

Those who live close to the high mountains
Are different from men along the rivers
And those on the intervales and cleared farms.
The mountain men know one another by signs,
And river men have their own kind of speech.
And strangest of all are the folks on islands

Who always hear the lapping of water
And see the tall scarlet cardinal flowers.
If an island man's children leave their home
They always return; they are drawn back.

Wilderness people are a special breed.
They have something that's not hearing or seeing
Reaching out from the mountains to touch them.

SHADDERS

Granny climbed up old Crane Mountain.
Neighbors told her not to go.
"Shadders pick on moonlight evenings;
Shadders watch the berries grow.

"Folks have seen 'em in fog-white moonlight,
Eyes as bright as a bat a-wing;
Hooty-owls calling, moles a-crawling;
We wouldn't go there for anything.

"Better climb the ridge to get blueberries."
Granny lit her pipe again;
Said, "I aim to do my picking
Where they're sweetest, on old Crane.

"Berries sweet as maple sapping,
Berries big as a green wild hop
Grow on the sides of old Crane Mountain;
I am to climb to the top—tip-top."

Granny clucked, set her pipe a-sparking,
Bright tin bucket flickin' in the sun,
Went on the mountain to pick blueberries,
Rounded a boulder and she was gone.

Didn't come back when night was sifting;
Didn't come back sun-up next day.
Neighbors said—who goes blueberrying
On old Crane has gone to stay.

Folks have seen her climbing with the shadders,
Filling her bucket in fog-white light;
Hooty-owls calling, moles a-crawling;
Picking blueberries on a moonlight night.

SHADBUSH

In May I climbed Crane Mountain
To the timberline's high edge
To see the shadbush blooming
Below each rocky ledge.

Then I climbed again for berries
That ripen there in June.
Clusters of crimson fruiting
Follow the early bloom.

There is no savor like them
As they crush upon my tongue.
They carry a magic with them,
And my heart is ever young.

Love came when the shadbush blossomed,
Love I still recall—
When the petals stir in springtime—
That did not meet the fall.

Let a shadbush mark my sleeping.
I may find love again
In a dream of one brief springtime—
Its glory and not its pain.

POVERTY GRASS

Silver white on the hillsides,
Leveled by winds that pass
When summer is ripe with glory,
Shines the silver "poverty grass."

Tangled with brake and "moonshine"
(The everlasting flower)
It covers the barren hillsides
Where the tall green spruces tower.

It springs with April's tricklings
On the rocks that lie below;
It dies in the heat of summer
Before autumn winds can blow.

All through the sultry August,
Silver color in the sun,
The slender spears stand like pale shades
Foreboding frost to come.

When winter's blasts sweep downwards
From off the mountain height
And bare the ragged places
Upspringing overnight,

We see the silver radiance,
This dead cold shining grass;
Between the drifts it gathers
Snow crystals as they pass.

And when the thaws are halted
By nights of freezing cold,
Each spear is bent, a bugle
Of ice with heart of gold.

Where this grass grows, there is no soil
To feed the roots of grain;

The cattle shun the silver slopes;
They know their search is vain.

Yet a forlorn wild beauty
Compensates those who see
These upland slopes when roaming
Old paths of memory.

THE APPLE-EATER

Cy Pritchad had heard about Johnny Appleseed
And how he went through the country leaving
A trail of apple trees. Cy followed his ways.
He had a big stomach for apple-eating.
He'd come to see you in the wintertime,
And when you brought up a pan of apples
(They kept perfect in those country cellars)
Cy would take out his pocket knife and pare
And eat a five-quart pan of apples.
He liked to go where folks had different kinds;
He like Seek-No-Furthers and Gill Flowers and Greenings,
Tolman Sweets and Russets, pippins and spice apples.
If you have a Sheep's Nose, he'd pick that one
First of all, for he wanted to get seeds.
He'd put the seeds into a little bag and thank you.
He put them in good places up north,
Here, there, and everywhere, on the roadside,
Beside old houses folks had left for good
And along rail fences where they could grow.

He lived long enough to see some of them
Come into bearing. Most were wild apples,
Hard and sour, not fit for eating.
But here and there among his plantings
Was a good apple; that red sweet apple
Back of the schoolhouse was one Cy planted.
Its scions are scattered all over the North Woods.
I don't know how many people grafted from it.

I miss going down cellar in winter
To fetch Cy a pan of winter apples.
Perhaps his planting didn't do much good,
But he was lucky to have one sweet apple
Out of all his seeds. Some folks don't have that much
Left from all their planting in this world.

MIS' COLE

She came walking up the road one morning
In late summer, slowly, taking her time.
She had on a blue calico wrapper,
Which was all the clothes I knew her to have.
Her face was still young, and her hair was tied back
With a leather thong cut from a tanned hide.
I called her in and made a cup of tea.
Then I asked her if anyone was sick.

"No," she said, "they're well. I'm leaving George.
I'm just walking away. Haying is done;
They can't say I left when the work was heavy.
Sarah is fourteen and Luddy twelve.
The twins are ten and Georgie is seven.
They can get along. I'm not coming back."
"Why, Mis' Cole," I said, "Don't say that. You know
You've got a man and five healthy children."

"I havent' got a single thing," she replied.
"Not even a hair ribbon, only leather
To tie my hair. I never have a cent.
Children are children; they have their own things.
I'm only hands and feet for George,
Someone to put the food on the table,
Someone to have more children for him,
And mend and hand-sew their dresses on them
Until they wear out in rags.
I'm walking to Pottersville this morning.

Then I don't know where I'll go; there must be
Better things than I've had in my life, somewhere.
I hope I'll find them. If they look for me
Tell the folks I'll never come back."

I went into the spare room and found
A blue hair ribbon. She took the leather thong
Off her hair and tied on the ribbon.
"It's the first one I've ever had,"
She said. "I'm beholden to you."
I packed a paper sack of victuals for her.
"Don't forget, you'll get hungry," I said.
"I'd hardly feel it, now I'm free, but I thank you.
If you ever find me, keep my secret.
They won't miss me, with the farm work,
And all the stock, and the trout brook,
And the beaver meadows, and the mountain.

"I was an orphan when I married George.
I never had no one or nobody, not even myself.
I have to find someone or something."
She went out, and I watched while she walked
Up the long Wilson Hill.

                    I heard where she was
Down below, but I said nothing.
George and the children got on all right.
It's long ago, but I think of her
And the leather strip in her yellow hair.

EZRA BROWN

There is one thing you always remember
About a man more than any other.
Sometimes it's a trick of his hand or eyes,
Or an old coat, or a dangling muffler;
And after a while in the neighborhood

A man comes to mean just that one queer thing
That sticks in the memory. I can see
Just one thing when I think of Ezra Brown—
His fingers fumbling at an old wallet
Trying to find a coin that wasn't there
To give to the needy. He spent his time
Trying to find God, and so his wallet
Had the worn lean look of a starved heifer,
And a dumb eloquence that chided him
For his own unworded reproachfulness
Of its shortcomings.

He had a passion
Than consumed him like a fire day by day:
It was to walk consciously with his God
As one might with a friend, to feel He entered
Into all the day's concerns large and small,
And was near so you could reach out to His hand
If sorrow or trouble came upon you.

Ezra died on his knees praying; we found him
Kneeling beside his bed one morning
With his head drooped on the patchwork bed-quilt,
Peaceful and quiet as a sleeping child.
He had wanted to be a preacher;
His father and grandfather before him
Thundered the gospel out of the pulpit;
Ezra wanted to follow their footsteps,
But someone had to stay and work the farm,
And so he gave up his hopes of preaching
And settled down to be a plain farmer.
There's his farm up there on the table land;
It looks like a green patch on the mountain.
I've wondered if his praying had to do
With his crops, for the drouth never killed them
And the frosts never troubled his uplands.
He prayed when he was clearing the timber
And kneeled in every freshly-turned furrow,
And beside charred stumps in the new clearings.
He swung the scythe and the buckwheat cradle
To the meter of the Psalms of David,
And set his flail flying at harvest time
To the hymns of Whitefield and Charles Wesley.

He cleared all his land and set out fruit trees,
Worsted nature until she was humble
And he could not feel her strong sullenness
Holding out against his crops and pastures.
The hard work was done; he could take life easy,
For the farm prospered and brought in the money
He enjoyed giving away to tramps that came beg-
      ging.
But right in the prime of life he lost heart
And his mind clouded. He used to tell us
He had lost God. He had made God his friend
So long that he couldn't live without Him.
He drove out to church regular and went forward
For prayers, but even that didn't help him.
Little by little we saw him going,
Broken, dumb-like, to that far country
That draws us surely when our work is done.

Ezra must have made believe he was God
Or a kind of steward, when he cleared the land
And grubbed stumps and made smooth fields
And planted them to rye and buckwheat and
      barley.
When he had finished his work polishing
The rough edges of nature the breath of life
Someway went out of him. I think likely
He had stopped *creating*; God never stops.
If Ezra had understood and had more strength
He would have pushed out farther into life
And not let God go on ahead of him.

LONELINESS

I

I cannot come again.
When spring buds forth,
I shall not wake to see
The sun turn north.

I am but flesh and blood.
Be pitiful and know—
I am not wind nor sun,
Nor rain nor the blown snow.

Here are my arms, my hands,
Here are my lips, my eyes:
Meeting with yours they find
All that is paradise.

II

Rain!—
Beating on the window pane
Lightly as a wind-whipped thread
Through the hours I lie abed—
Who would have thought that I
Should love your whimpering cry
Better than bright sunlight driven
From the deep blue courts of heaven?

Leaves!—
Swinging high against the eaves,
With a whispering sound that rides
On the wind like far off tides—
Who would have thought that I
Should wake to hear your cry
With quick tears that you made less
The pain of my loneliness?

Wind!—
Shrilling at the broken blind,
Baying like a sullen hound
Night's still quarry from the ground—
Who would have thought that I
Laughed aloud to hear your cry,
Laughed because you shut from me
Dreams of all that cannot be?

III

The winds blow as they list,
And love goes where it will,

And I would go where my heart is
And sit on a lonely hill —

A lonely hill where slow rain falls
And the brown leaves bend and drip,
And I would drink with the brown leaves
The rain-drops, sip by sip.

And I would lay me down with them
When they fall upon the ground
One by one, the whole night long
With a hollow rustling sound.

And I would sleep with the brown leaves
Nor know that winter came,
Nor see the sun upon the snow —
An iris of blue flame.

I would sleep well and wake at last
At the melting of the snow,
Drowsy-eyed, until the sun
Had warmed me with its glow.

Clean of body and clean of heart . . .
Then, never remembering
Love, or you, I would rise and go
And follow the feet of Spring.

NANCE HILLS

A Lumber Camp Idyll

The lumber camps were lonely years ago.
I've heard my mother tell how many a time,
When she was "keeping Shanty" years ago
In the North Woods, cooking three meals a day
For twenty men on Morgan lumber jobs,

That four months would go by, and she'd not see
Another woman, and she would grow wan
And half forgetful out of loneliness,
And have strange fancies coming and start quick
If icicles fell down from off the eaves;
And if a panther howled down in the swamp
She'd go and bar the door, although she knew
'Twould never come into the clearing there.
And then she'd always say, "'Twas not so bad
In later years, for then I had the boys
Playing around to keep me company,
And never went clean crazy like Nance Hills,
Who kept the Byrd Pond Shanty at 'The Forks.'
'Twas good six miles away as the crow flies
Across the cedar swamp to reach Byrd Pond,
Yet Nance would often tramp the trail and come
And sit with me what time she had to spare,
And play with you an hour with blocks and things
When you were little. And one day she said:

"'I'm not the same since little Jimmie died;
You see, he was the only one I had.
I ache somewhere; I think it's in my heart,
And I've steeped herbs, but still the pain don't go.
When I went home last year, I told Mis' Tripp,
And she said: "Sho, don't worry about that;
I've felt that way now, years and years ago
When I was young and lost a little child.
It's *baby-fever*; when you've lost your own,
Or they've been grown up for a heap of years,
Or sometimes when you're just sick and alone,
The spell comes on; you sit and ache and ache
And don't know rightly where. Sometimes it
     seems
Your heart is jumping right up in your throat,
And other times as if a lump of lead
Lay on your breast, and you have crazy dreams
Of babies; and sometimes in broad daylight
You see one come and play round on the floor,
And food don't taste, and you can't even cry;
But always you know somehow what you want,
And feel soft fingers clutching at your breast,

And all night long a head upon your arm.
That's 'baby-fever'; it drives women mad."

"She sat a time, and then she spoke again:
'I've hoped and hoped since little Jimmie died —'
then I just bustled out and stirred the fire
And made her drink a good hot cup of tea.

"One day I heard our 'marker' laugh and say,
'They've got a baby over at "The Forks."'
And I said, 'No, I haven't heard of it.'
And he said, 'Yep, it's so, for I looked in:
There was a cradle rocking on the floor.'

"'Poor thing,' I said; 'she must have had a time
Without a woman 'round to care for her;
I must go over there the first fair day.'
Next day I saddled our old skidding horse
And strapped a blanket on, and rode the trail
Through Cedar Swamp and came down to 'The
        Forks.'

"Nance met me at the Shanty door; her face
Was sunshine. 'Sh-h-h,' she said, 'he's gone to
        sleep.
Take off your shawl; your mittens are all stiff;
I'll thaw them out; sit down and warm yourself.'
We sat down by the stove and talked and talked,
And all the while she stitched and laughed away
And showed me fixings such as women make.

"I asked to see the baby and Nance said,
'If you don't mind today, I'll let him sleep,
For he was sick and fretted in the night.'
I thought 'twas queer I couldn't look at him,
But something in her face kept my tongue still.
I rode off home and she stood watching me
Out of the clearing. I can see her now,
With her red hair wrapped in a bright blue shawl;
She looked like some old picture I had seen
I think now rightly in a Cath'lic Church;
They're full of pictures and of idols too.

"The snow was deep that year; I couldn't go
Until Spring came again, on the swamp trail,
And by that time I'd heard no one had seen
The baby that was over at 'The Forks.'
They couldn't get a word out of Nance's man.
He'd say black oaths whenever they quizzed him.
But when Nance was alone—a man had watched—
She'd bring the baby from her own bunk-room
And coddle it, and nurse it at her breast.
But no one ever heard it make a cry.

"One day when the Spring freshets gullied out
The old log roads, Jim Hills came riding in.
'Can you come over? Nance is awful sick,'
He said as soon as I had let him in.
I said I could, and got on up behind.

We had to walk the horse through ankle slush,
And when we got there Nance was awful sick,
And wild with fever. 'Land,' said I, 'what's this?
She needs a woman; let me look at her.'
And when I made her easy, I went out
To tend the baby, for I saw a crib.
You won't believe 'twas true: I turned the quilt
And saw a baby made of cloth and rags—
A poor rag doll that she had dressed and nursed
And *made believe with* to her starved out heart.
I stared at it and lifted up the thing. —
I'd swear that it was warm—and then I screamed
And let it drop, for somehow something moved
Just like a baby moves, right in my hands.
And then I put it back, for Nance cried out,
And I heard Jim come blundering in the house.

"He saw me by the crib and said shamefaced:
'I couldn't stop her; so I held my tongue.'
'Of course,' I said; then Nance screamed out again,
And I went out and put the kettle on
To have hot water in a little while.

"She slept at last, and nestling by her side
I laid her baby—the real living one

That came to answer that old craving need
That's deep in women. When the wind blew in
The chinks between the logs, I slipped away
And brought her old blue shawl to wrap her in
Against the cold. Then Jim came tip-toe soft.
'She's gone to sleep; don't you wake her,' I said.
'I won't,' he whispered; then he turned to me:
'She looks like someone, but I don't know who—
I think my mother, but I don't just know.'

"Just then we heard the log chains clank outside.
The men had come; the skidding horses raced
Down to the barn; the kitchen door banged wide;
'Hullo,' a big voice called; 'say, where's the
    grub?'"

FLINT

I never believed they were married lovers:
He was such a hard man—and she was hard;
Both Presbyterians, and old-fashioned
Enough to think that bodies can damn souls,
And that original sin can shake us
From the Tree of Life into perdition.

I thought their marriage was just a bargain
They had made because they thought it a duty.
They never called each other by first names.
'Twas always "Mr." and "Mrs."—stiff words
For the breakfast table, year in and year out.
But one could see they never flinched from life.
They worked hard and brought up thirteen children.
Most of them went to college: they believed
The Lord commanded men to get knowledge.
Abial, the eldest, became a preacher;
Ichabod went off somewhere engineering;
Mary taught school; now she's at a college

Where they teach girls to be missionaries
And send them out to heathen in China;
Bethuel is a doctor down in Utica.
They're all off somewhere working out salvation,
And the old folks live on in the farm house
And use their religion as a ramrod
To stiffen their spines, so they can hold out
Until death against all the natural
Human happiness that they're so scared of.

But I changed my mind about them last year.
I had brought some candy up from the store.
I stopped in at their house—neighbors were
        there—
And passed the candy—just peppermint sticks
With pink stripings—the kind that children like.
Somehow I missed him when I passed it,
And I had just enough sticks to go around
Without him. Well, I thought nothing of it:
A man don't set much store by candy—
(I had forget they felt it was a sin
To waste money on such foolish notions
As candy, so he hardly knew its taste,)
I sat near the outside door behind them,
And I saw her hand slip back of her chair
And find his hand, while she kept on talking,
And when it drew back he had the candy.
She couldn't bear to have the little treat
And feel that he was not sharing it too.

It was a simple thing—but it held all
The love we had thought they were missing.
Their hardness was only a cloak—a mask
To hide their rich treasure from the curious;
And I understood then why their children
Had grown up like young trees, strong and lovely.

Now I've a fondness when I'm teaming it
For eating pink-striped peppermint candy;
I think—when I'm munching along the road
And flicking the heads of the timothy
With my whip—"They loved one another—

We were so blind; they loved hard all the time.
Their natures were flint; there's bound to be fire
When you strike flint. They poured out a great
    love
Into life; maybe that was the secret
Old John Calvin tried so hard to teach us."

Lucia Newell Oliviere

Lucia Newell Oliviere

The facts of Lucia Newell Oliviere's life are sparse. Until now she has appeared dimly as the mother of the poet Jeanne Robert Foster. Oliviere herself was an aspiring poet and was probably in no small way responsible for her daughter's impulse to write. Side by side, their works and lives provide a gloss on the way that mother's and daughter's visions create each other.

Oliviere was born and christened Lucinda Newell in North River just before the Civil War. She was one of four daughters of a white-water man who drowned in the Hudson at North River on a log drive. She stood with her mother and sisters on the bank, unable to help him as he lost his grip on a rock and slipped away. The daughters were adopted out, and Lucia was taken into the home of the Reverend Enos and Sybil Putnam in Johnsburg, the same family who would later take in her own daughter Jeanne. Putnam was a Wesleyan Methodist minister who had kept a station on the underground railroad, hiding slaves in his cellar. Lucinda, known as Lizzy while she lived with the Putnams, was imbued with the tenets of civil rights, a belief that sustained her in the feminist and human rights movements years later.

Lucia attended Albany Normal School and taught school in Peekskill and Elmira before becoming principal of the village school at Chestertown. Her marriage to Frank Oliver, a lumberman, and the birth of her four children kept her rooted to the Adirondacks until, with the depression in the mountain economy of the 1890s, her husband moved to Glens Falls to work as a carpenter. Lucia was happy at last to be in a place that offered what she thought of as cultural stimulation for her and her children but at the same time suffered the loss of her daughter Jeanne in marriage. Soon after, the family moved to Schenectady where Lizzy again changed her name, this time to "Lucia," and altered her married surname to "Oliviere." In Schenectady she became an active writer and lecturer on human rights and a pioneer suffragist, using her own home as a center for invited speakers, organizing, and canvasing voters. She joined the Socialist Party, which admitted women on equal footing with men, and twice ran for state senator on that party's ticket. She labored diligently and publicly for the common good, accomplishing some signal victories for working people. Her campaign on behalf of the underpaid women janitors at the General Electric plant in Schenectady resulted in their being included in a settlement made by the War Labor Board.

One of the things of which she was most proud was, of course, her daughter Jeanne who became a famous beauty, journalist, poet and successful social worker. Oliviere recognized her eldest daughter's outstanding gifts and urged Jeanne to develop them and go where they would take her, knowing that it would carry her beyond the mountains. Lucia depended on her daughter for companionship and labor, especially in winter when her husband was away in lumber camps, and Jeanne took on some of the extra work. But the mother also relied on Jeanne to fulfill the promise that her own gifts and aspirations found thwarted. Jeanne was to be all that Lucia, bound by birth and marriage, had resigned herself to renouncing. She referred to Jeanne as her favorite, her chosen child, investing in the girl her own hope for a life that transcended in spirit the rocky existence she had as the wife of a mountain man. Her letters to Jeanne are insistently religious, even Biblical in their rhythms, and grounded in Christology. Many of them read like meditations which are merely shared with one who would understand them. One written on New Year's Day in 1909 is typical:

> I pray for you my dearest—on the eve of this New Year—as I do on all other eves—that your soul may hear a call to some earnest life work. That some heavenly visions may come to your heart, with its dazzling light shutting out all lesser groveling aims. You have talents—you were born to teach—to instruct others—I hope you will find your spiritual wings, and rise out of and above earth's vanities. Why should we who are immortal wear the obsession of things which belong to clay. Is a little handful of dust worth so much thought?[1]

The passage hints at the spiritualism and mysticism that recurs in her letters. Like her daughter, she found her way beyond the strict protestantism of her family to a broader definition of Christianity and spirituality. Yet this is an oddly transcendental message from a woman whose own concerns were so earth-bound. Her work with the Socialist Party, with its program of social reform, obviously satisfied her own need to do "earnest work," something that would benefit others who were struggling with hardship here and now. At the same time, however, Lucia was working at a more private labor, writing poetry and fiction. There remains an unpublished novel set in Johnsburg during the Civil War and an assortment of sketches and brief fictional pieces in manuscript suggesting that Oliviere was, like her daughter, wrestling with her muse for many years. At her death in 1927 she had prepared a collection of her poems which she hoped to see published. A year later Jeanne, by then an established writer, edited the poems and saw them published in *Old Houses*. Most of what is said about Foster's poetry applies as well to her mother's as it appeared in this volume. The free verse captures the clipped ver-nacular of regional speech and unravels the narratives that show tough-willed characters making their peace with the mountains and themselves. Lucia Newell Oliviere, like her daughter after her, could not deny the poetry bred into her by her early life in the Adirondacks.

THE STAGE DRIVER

I rode up to Spruce Lake every year
With Roland Bennet.
He told me he had "drove the stage for twenty-
    five years."
He was a quiet man with deep-set blue eyes.
Made me think of a Scotchman I had known.
Every year he asked me questions
About the world I knew—cities and mountains
    and prairies,
And the ocean I had crossed.
He had "never been anywhere 'cept here," he
    said,
So I fell into the habit of bringing him

Every summer, a book of travels.
He always talked to me about
The things he had read in those books.
Once something broke in the harness,
And we stopped at his place for repairs.
A coarse, blowsy woman and three half-grown
     boys
Stared curiously at me.
The woman stopped her work
(She was getting dinner) to ask:
"Are you the man that gives Roland books?
(Glancing at a homemade bookcase nailed to the
     wall.)
They hurt him; he reads them when he should
     be working
Raising potatoes and corn for me and the chil-
     dren.
There's many a time he forgets the cows and
     the pigs
Reading them 'ere books.
Oh, they are locked up, all right.
(As I started to open the bookcase.)
He wouldn't let one of us touch 'em—
Not that any of us want to;
We have something more sensible to do.
I believe they will be the death of him yet.
Why, sometimes he talks in his sleep
Of the strange places he has read about.
I sure have a hard time bringing up a family,
And I *could* have married Silas Burch;
He rides in his own automobile,
And his wife had silk dresses
And a hired girl.
He's a widower now—she died last Christmas."
Just then Roland came in.
Declining the invitation to dinner, we started
For the lake, five miles beyond;
He was silent, seemed to be wondering
What I thought about things.
He knew what his wife had been telling me.
At last I spoke:
"When the harvest is over
And things are prepared for the winter,

Suppose you take a vacation.
I am going to the coast;
You can come along as handy man;
Expenses and a little besides,
As much as you would earn driving stage this
    winter."
The reins shook in his hand,
His face was illumined,
The fire within shone through the flesh.
As we neared the lake Roland spoke;
His lips were ashen white:
"Thank you, but I am a religious man,
And must ask direction."
The painted leaves of autumn were falling
When I saw Roland again.
He was taking me to the station.
He was different now.
There was something finer and nobler about him;
He had fought the battle
With his own soul and won.
As he took my traps from the wagon I said:
"Well, Roland, are you coming with me to see
   · the world?"
He stopped, removed his cap
As if in reverence to something unseen.
"I can't do it—I can't do it.
My soul has been going all over the world for
    years
While my body has been penned up here.
My soul is free—free as God's air
Or the birds that have wings,
But my body is bound by the words I have spoken
The deeds I have done.
If I went out after my soul—
Can't you understand?—
I should never return, and I should be accursed
    forever.
There are many things I don't understand,
But I know that one's deeds and words
Are fetters and chains that imprison.
Once I saw a man who had committed some
    great crime
Dragging a ball and chain. I am like that man.

If I go with you I would never return,
And wherever my soul drew me
I would drag that ball and chain of things left
    undone."
Tears dimmed the fire in his eyes.
I said good-bye with a feeling that here
Was something finer than I had known.
The accumulated desires of a man's body
Had burned out to a white ash,
Leaving him stainless.

.   .   .   .

Two years later, when I came again,
One of Roland's boys drove the stage.
"Father is dead—we found him
Last fall lying under a maple tree,
One of the books you gave him
In his hand. Mother says they killed him.
She's married now to Silas Burch.
I reckon she's not grieving much.
We boys live on the old place.
She's too stuck up to care for us.
Sometimes I read father's books.
We didn't understand him, or he us.
He was beautiful as he lay there
With the red maple leaves upon him.
He looked young like a boy, and he was smiling.
Here we are at Spruce Lake. Come to see us
And I will show you where he died.
I've fenced the tree around
And I often sit there on Sunday
With one of his books, trying to understand
The things he did."

THE LINE FENCE

Celia Wilson had been angling for Ike Warner
'Nigh onto ten years.
The gossips said Celia never would land him

But here was the wedding day
And we were not invited,
All on account of a line fence.
Ike 'lowed it was a foot over on his land,
So one night Ike and Joe Harp (his hired man)
Moved it a foot over unto us.
Father waited until Ike had gone to camp meet-
    ing
Then father moved it back.
(Ike sets a store by religion
Every fall at camp meeting he gets sanctified),
But father says horse sense and honesty
Are good enough for him.
When Ike saw what father had done
While he was at camp meeting praying
The Lord to protect him and his'n,
He got black in the face,
—But Joe Harp cussed a blue streak,
(He had no call to be pious
Seeing he never owned any land
Or ever expected to).
So he used all the cuss words
He had learned lumbering and canaling
And a few others, over that line fence
That wouldn't stay put.
Father sat over on "Hog's Back" and laughed
To hear Joe Harp cuss over other people's calam-
    ities.

That night the fence caught fire and burned down.
It caught from Ike Warner's own fallow
So there the matter rested.
And now Ike Warner was to be married and we
    were not invited.
I knew mother was grieved
For a wedding or a funeral is a real treat
To country folks who have few pleasures
And mother is a master hand at weddings and
    funerals.
She can make a three story wedding cake
Or lay out a corpse better
Then any woman in Warren country.
Father took the hoe and went to the back lot.

Mother said she 'spected he wanted to be alone
And hated to see the wedding folks go by.
For Celia *would* be married in church.
Mother and I sat down to sew carpet rags.
I knew mother was thinking of what she had
          missed,
The women talking about births and deaths
And the season's pickling,
The sly jokes over the bride and groom
And the bride's presents, and wondering
If Celia would be a good worker,
For Ike was tight fisted
And wouldn't stand for help in the kitchen.

At last mother spoke:
"I wonder if it's a love match?"
"I can't imagine a woman loving a man after
          seeing him around ten years.
It's toleration most likely and itching for a home
And children of her own to fuss over."
A clanking of chains broke in our talk
Billy, father's prize Cotswold ram, had broken
          his tether.
Just then round the sharp turn of the road
By the old log barn that grandfather built,
The heads of Ike Warner's bay colts appeared.
At the sight of Billy primed for war,
They reared and plunged sideways off the bank.
Father was on the spot before Ike had time to
          disentangle himself.
He had been setting in the log barn all the time
Waiting to see Ike go by.
Ike wasn't hurt but Celia had fainted from fright
So while Ike was righting up things
And Joe Harp cussing the ram
Father carried Celia to the house
And laid her on the couch in the best room.
While mother was fussing over Celia
Giving her peppermint tea and such like
Father took Ike to the kitchen, to get some
          cider.

There is something in hard cider
That mellows up the heart and wipes out old
    grudges.

Father spoke first:
"Darn that ram!
Shake, Ike, I'll go halves and build the line fence
Just where you say it ought to be."
But Ike, after taking another drink of cider,
Grabbed father's hand and said:
"We're two dum fools! We don't need any line
    fence;
You just cut the grass as far as you think is yourn
And by Gosh, I'll take what's left."
After Celia come to
Ike said: "Now neighbors, put on your jockeys,
And come along to the wedding dinner."
Mother gave Celia a pair of blue and white
Flannel blankets grandmother wove.
Mother set a store by them,
And father slipped a ten dollar gold piece into
    Celia's hand
(Father was close fisted, too).
When we were setting down to dinner
We missed Joe Harp, the hired man.
Pretty soon he came in all tousled and het up.
    He looked mad.
He burst out: "I have been chasing that cussed
    ram;
I got the best of him at last
And he's tethered to an oak tree."
Father said: "That ram cost me fifty dollars clean
    cash.
I wouldn't take a thousand for him today."

So that's how there come to be a row of black-
    berry bushes
Where that fence used to be.
Blackberry briars love to follow fire tracks,
And the only contention now is—

Whose wife makes the best pie and blackberry
      jam.
There isn't a lazy hair in Celia's head.
She and Ike get along scrumptious.
Mother says she believes it *was* a love match after
      all.

BETHEL

He brought her to me on an early summer twi-
      light.
The fleecy June clouds floating before the wind
Made drifting shadows over the meadows
And the tall poplars' silvery leaves were haloed
      with the setting sun.
He said with a coarse laugh,
"Bethel thinks she's sick—
Wants to get away from me
And her work I reckon.
There was a boarder last year
That 'shined up' to her—
One of the gentleman kind.
I'm not afraid of him for *he's dead*.
Keep her a while
'Till she gets foolish notions out of her head.
Then she'll be glad to come back to her bread
      and butter.
She's just plumb selfish,
Leaving me with all the chores to do.
The neighbors sent a doctor.
He said she must have a change,
Lord knows what for.
I don't need any change,
But I've brought her to you
Seeing you're a relation.
I can't afford to pay money out for her,
But I'll bring things,

Maple sirup and dried apples
And her strawberry jam.
She made it for the boarder last summer.
She coughs just like he did.
I'd say she's pining for him, instead of being
An honest virtuous wife.
Well, so long, I must be going."
He stopped at the gate, looking back.
"I just don't know how I'll get on.
Haying's coming and no woman
To milk, feed calves and pigs
And rake after—besides getting meals."
I looked at Bethel, her eyes were fixed
On the hilltops, where the sunshine
Still lingered.
I wondered much what strange
Complexity of life
Had brought these two human beings together,
A dolt, heavy and dull
As the clod beneath his feet,
And a bit of earth's sunshine,
A radiant soul—heaven's light in her eyes.
I looked at Bethel. Hers was a face
Of Divine Peace. The last rays of day
Aureoled her head.
She spoke. "Has he gone? And may I stay
Here with you as long as— —?"
Here her voice drifted away
And became indistinct.
But she looked at me with smiling eyes.

The sultry days of summer passed.
Bethel grew thinner and weaker.
She never spoke of home or of the clod
Who owned her. She talked much
Of life, death and the hereafter.
Here serenity was wonderful.
Only once did she speak freely. She asked
"Do you think I'll be gone when he comes?
I can't go back to him. Once I had a lamb—
The ewe died.
I mothered it until it was like a child to me,

(I have never given birth).
It was harvest time. I struggled with him
For the life of the lamb,
He wanted it for meat.
I snatched it away from him.
Then he struck me with his clenched fist.
When I awoke, still lying where I fell,
It was dark, and he was gone.
A trickle of blood was on my white dress
And on my lips.
Since then I have not been living with him.
My body was there, but my soul
Has been far away in the sunshine."
At the first reddening of autumn leaves
He came. Bethel was sleeping.
I went to call her
But she had slipped the leash of flesh;
She was done with earth's clods forever.

MARY JANE

Mary Jane had lived long past her allotted three
    score and ten;
She was not weary of life. Having been well
    cared for,
She was still strong and supple.
Chaperoned in youth, and more so in her old age,
She thirsted for freedom.
It was irksome in youth to be guarded
When adventure waited at every corner,
And one's heart was throbbing with Desire.
But in old age when one has nothing to fear from
    Adventure
And Desire sleeps in the graveyard with Hope,
When all the bright dreams of youth are thin
    ghosts
Remembered only in that lone hour of the night

That comes just before daybreak
Then, when one is old and weary, longing for
   freedom,
It was detestable, to have not only her own
   family,
But all the neighbors out of sheer kindness,
Trying to chaperone her coming in and going
   out.
So when Bessie, her daughter-in-law, whom she
   had never loved overmuch,
Told her with a show of emotion, that her *passing*
   was near,
Mary Jane simply said:
"Are you or any of the family going along?
If not, I think it will be a rather enjoyable ad-
   venture.
It will be the first chance I have had, to go any-
   where *alone*."

WINTER

Winter is here,
I hear his padded footsteps at the door
While yet I dream in soft content
Before the pine knot fire.
I see his hand upon the window pane,
Surpassing far the witchery of flame;
I hear the shingles burst apart
At touch of icy fingers;
On stormy winds I see his form fly by,
His face fantastic gleams,
His eyes—hail-tipped—
Like dewdrops glisten;
And as from roofs of deep earth caverns,
Stalactites hang from every hair of head and
   beard,
His garments are of ice,

With fleece of snowy crystals;
As polar bear walking upright he seems.
I love him not,
And yet he is so wondrous strong,
Majestic, beautiful
Even in his terror.

SPRING SONGS

THE CROCUS

Step lightly for I feel
    The earth's pulse quicken.
It is the crocus 'neath her heart;
    It struggles upward
From the mold,
To kiss the sunshine of the spring.

THE BLUE BIRD

I heard the sweet sap
    Trickling everywhere;
I saw the waters break
    From ice-bound caverns;
And then a bird bluer than the sky
Tapped at my window,
    And afar I heard a robin
Shyly trilling—"Spring is here."

Adelaide Crapsey

Adelaide Crapsey

It would be reductive to classify Adelaide Crapsey as an Adirondack writer, but she is rightly included in this collection. The fact is that her two finest contributions to American poetry — her best verses and the creation of the cinquain — were produced during the year she spent secluded at a Saranac Lake cure cottage, those months just preceding her death from tuberculosis. It is widely accepted that the death she saw lurking just beyond the bedstead and her own proclivity for repression and compression combined to wrench from her the poetic achievement of her last year. However, one ought not dismiss or underestimate the impact of those seasons spent in the region's grip, with its bleak aura of illness and despair.

Crapsey was a New Yorker by birth, although her upbringing and subsequent travels abroad made her a citizen of a much larger and less parochial world. Born in Brooklyn Heights in 1878, she was one of eleven children of the Reverend Algernon Crapsey, an Episcopal clergyman, and Adelaide Trowbridge. Within a year of her birth, the family moved to Rochester, New York, where her father became rector of St. Andrew's. After attending public schools in Rochester, Adelaide was sent to Kemper Hall boarding school in Wisconsin where she studied with the Episcopal nuns. She distinguished herself academically in Latin and French while she demonstrated an enduring enthusiasm for women's basketball and edited the school magazine. She graduated as valedictorian and, after a brief interlude with her family, went on to study at Vassar where she determined to be a teacher, one of the few professions open to bright young women. At Vassar she was chosen class poet for three years and edited the college yearbook. Again she excelled academically and graduated with honors. At the age of twenty-four she returned to Kemper Hall to teach, but debilitating fatigue — an early symptom of her disease — began to haunt her. Up to that point, her life had largely been defined by her association with women's schools, as both student and teacher. While this limited her experience of the world, it afforded her the opportunity to explore an enormous literary domain with the support and encouragement of other professional women scholars. She began, under this benign influence, to see herself as a scholar. The verses she had been writing since she was a child were tucked away while Crapsey's intellectual pursuits flourished. The poetic nature in her was trained on the study of prosody which she was beginning: poetry surfaced only sporadically and casually. During the following years she travelled, worked, and studied in Europe, returning home to support her father during his heresy trial in Batavia in 1905.

Crapsey's relationship with her father was the most intense and significant in her life in the bustling household. Their intellectual and emotional rapport was singular for both of them. In his autobiography, her father mentions only one of his children by name, and that is Adelaide. His heresy was born out of a social conscience which recoiled from the materialism and elitism of the church as he saw it. The move to Rochester had been an ethical show of concern with reform and relief, a gesture that forced his growing family to live in reduced circumstances but within an energetic and challenging Christianity. That latitude in thinking led him to deliver a sermon in which he addressed the incredibility of the Virgin Birth. His latitudinarian views must have infused the young mind of Adelaide and given her permission to find her own individual way in spiritual and intellectual matters.

After her father's suspension from the church, Adelaide took a job teaching at a preparatory school in Connecticut. By then, her undetected disease was advanced enough that she often had to spend weekends in bed to recover from the rigors of the week's teaching. Still she rallied the energy to accompany her father to the Hague Peace Conference and on a walking tour of Wales in 1907. Her health remained so weak, however, that she finally resigned her teaching post and sailed for Europe. Over the next three years she pursued what she thought to be her life-work, a study of English metrics and prosody. Her days were a patchwork of poverty, ill-health, haphazard living arrangements and tedious labor in a reading room, none of which was suited to a young woman afflicted with tuberculosis. When she finally returned to America in 1911 she was accorded an instructorship in poetics at Smith College in Northampton, Massachusetts. Her commitment to her study in metrics was complete:

when she wasn't teaching or in bed resting, she was sitting in an airless room of the college library counting syllables and stresses or occasionally copying her own poems.

At about that time she began dressing entirely in gray—hat, cape, dress, even shoes—an affectation which has several possible explanations. It is tempting to speculate on just why she adopted such a singular mode of dress, even though the poet herself cautioned that every individual has the right "to unexplained acts and motives,"[1] and we should perhaps not probe too deeply. Certainly such apparel signalled a renunciation of fashion, ironically creating a distinctive style even as she shunned it. Almost a nun-like choice of habit, it may also have been part of her attempt at economy. It was likewise a gesture of individuation, a sign of distinction not unlike Emily Dickinson's donning of white. Crapsey's inborn and nurtured individualism—like her father's—enabled her to throw off fashion in clothing, manners and intellectual habits. There was also in her personality a tendency to restraint. In some sense this mannerism of wearing only gray was like her own experimentation and invention of the cinquain. Her minimalist dress is, in this light, a metaphor for the restraint and compression one finds in the later poems. Even her features bore the signs of her conflicting impulses: her full mouth, deepset eyes, and strong chin suggest a character darkly sensuous and determined to weigh intellect over feeling. During her years at Smith College, she was experimenting with the cinquain, a poetic form characterized by unrhymed, five-line verses based on an accent pattern which works up to and falls away from a climax in the fourth line. It is a form that employs great "technical restraint and extreme compression."[2] Critics and literary historians have noted her mastery of the form as well as her intellectual independence. She showed herself to be ultimately a modern poet in her use of Oriental technique, the absence of Christian certainties, and the use of the lyric for personal, nearly confessional, statement.[3] Indeed, she was the unconscious precursor of the Imagist poets.

That summer her chronic malaise was finally diagnosed as tuberculin meningitis which it was supposed was affecting the lining of her brain. A year later, while on vacation in the Berkshire Mountains, she collapsed and was put into a Pittsfield hospital. After a few weeks, during which she admitted the nature of her illness to her family and friends, she was taken to a cure cottage in Saranac Lake where she was

attended to by Dr. Baldwin, one of Trudeau's own cured consump-
tives. During the last year of her life, the year at Saranac Lake, she
wrote many of the poems that appeared in the posthumously published edition of her *Verse*, and she perfected the cinquain form. The
volume on English prosody was essentially finished. Ironically the
genius who had believed herself to be a scholar first and poet second
was to be remembered for her achievement in verse form.

Her letters during that time contrast strikingly with the poems
penned from the same bed. The former are cheerful, optimistic and
brave. Even when faced with the inevitability of her invalidism, she
could write to a friend:

> if its chronic tuberculosis why thats what it is and I'm just going to go
> ahead, find a way of living thats as little invalidish as possible, get what I
> can out of things and let it go at that.[4]

Crapsey was no ethereal, disembodied wraith spinning out wisps of
poetry. She was a vigorous young woman, bold of mind as well as
body. At Kemper Hall and Vassar she had been active in basketball as
both player and referee; she had walked over Europe and Wales; she
celebrated the body's delight in movement and sensuality. In many
of the poems, including some of the final ones like "Amaze," there is
a startling physicality and sensuality not wholly derived from the
literary models she used. How much more painful it must have been
for a young woman used to activity, even half of her time, to contemplate a life confined to bed and hours of complete physical passivity.
Her response in the poems is the kind of visceral anger one finds in
"To the Dead in the Grave-Yard Under My window." What's missing
in the poems and the letters both is any Christian emphasis on recon-
ciliation, atonement, or anticipation of eternity. It is as though
Crapsey, in her individualism and latitudinarian faith, shunned any
belief in the Hereafter. The poems of this period are rueful and
bleak, the product of a consciousness which sees itself facing death
and nothing beyond. Her liberal Christianity is depicted here in the
unsentimental lyric "The Entombment."

The closer death came, the brighter her genius burned. The
romantic notion that consumption liberated the poetic spirit seems to

have some basis in medical fact. The fever which is symptomatic of the disease and the imposed physical inactivity sometimes led the patient to heightened emotional awareness and mental activity, to the kind of sensitivity which might yield — from a nascent poet — her best work. Certainly the cinquain form mimics her life with its rising intensity abruptly cut off in the terminal image. The Saranac poems are newer and fresher than the earlier ones which were more literary in inspiration and manner. Crapsey seems to have known this and had prepared for publication a clutch of what she believed were the best of them. In February, a dark season in the Adirondacks when the world is gripped with cold, Crapsey finished the first poem included here, "Lines Written to My Left Lung." She had endured three failed attempts at pneumothorax, a procedure in which a hollow needle was inserted between two of the patient's ribs so gas could be injected into the body cavity to collapse a diseased lung so that it could rest. Looking beyond her window to the cemetery or "Trudeau's garden," she was stirred to the dark humor and bitter denial of these poems. Forbidden to work more on her metrical study, she turned to her own poetry in earnest. The result includes most of the pieces here.

As a teacher, she was remembered as having a passion for form and a reverence for technique, believing that form, not feeling, made beauty.[5] In the final months of her life, form and feeling coalesced into the gem-like poems which follow. In August of 1914 she was looking for another health resort to move to, one less expensive and arctic. She had asked her dearest woman friend to buy her pastel, flowered dressing gowns, an important departure for the woman in gray, saying "I've had so many just plain colors."[6] Her impulse to compression and concision, expressed at Smith in her gray habit, was finding its expression in the poems. The thirty-six year old poet reached out with the last whisper of life in her to embrace a gentler aesthetic. In August she took the train to Rochester for a visit with her family before moving to another sanatorium. The fetid summer air accelerated her illness; in October she died at home. Her ashes were interred, with poetry and ceremony to mark the place, in Mount Hope Cemetery in Rochester. Some peculiar circumstances surrounding the publication of her poems after her death, including spirit messages purported to come from Adelaide to assist her editor, suggest to some that Crapsey may have been wrong about eternity.

TO THE DEAD IN THE GRAVE-YARD UNDER MY WINDOW: — WRITTEN IN A MOMENT OF EXASPERATION

How can you lie so still? All day I watch
And never a blade of all the green sod moves
To show where restlessly you toss and turn,
And fling a desperate arm or draw up knees
Stiffened and aching from their long disuse;
I watch all night and not one ghost comes forth
To take its freedom of the midnight hour.
Oh, have you no rebellion in your bones?
The very worms must scorn you where you lie,
A pallid mouldering acquiescent folk,
Meek habitants of unresented graves.
Why are you there in your straight row on row
Where I must ever see you from my bed
That in your mere dumb presence iterate
The text so weary in my ears: "Lie still
And rest; be patient and lie still and rest."
I'll not be patient! I will not lie still!
There is a brown road runs between the pines,
And further on the purple woodlands lie,
And still beyond blue mountains lift and loom;
And I would walk the road and I would be
Deep in the wooded shade and I would reach
The windy mountain tops that touch the clouds.
My eyes may follow but my feet are held.
Recumbent as you others must I too
Submit? Be mimic of your movelessness
With pillow and counterpane for stone and sod?
And if the many sayings of the wise
Teach of submission I will not submit
But with a spirit all unreconciled
Flash an unquenched defiance to the stars.
Better it is to walk, to run, to dance,
Better it is to laugh and leap and sing,
To know the open skies of dawn and night,
To move untrammel'd down the flaming noon,

And I will clamour it through weary days
Keeping the edge of deprivation sharp,
Nor with the pliant speaking on my lips
Of resignation, sister to defeat.
I'll not be patient. I will not lie still.

And in ironic quietude who is
The despot of our days and lord of dust
Needs but, scarce heeding, wait to drop
Grim casual comment on rebellion's end:
"Yes; yes . . . *Wilful and petulant but now*
As dead and quiet as the others are."
And this each body and ghost of you hath heard
That in your graves do therefore lie so still.

Saranac Lake—
November—1913

THE IMMORTAL RESIDUE
INSCRIPTION FOR MY VERSE

Wouldst thou find my ashes? Look
In the pages of my book;
And as these thy hand doth turn,
Know here is my funeral urn.

AMAZE

I know
Not these my hands
And yet I think there was
A woman like me once had hands
Like these.

THE LONELY DEATH

In the cold I will rise, I will bathe
In waters of ice; myself
Will shiver, and shrive myself,
Alone in the dawn, and anoint
Forehead and feet and hands;
I will shutter the windows from light,
I will place in their sockets the four
Tall candles and set them a-flame
In the grey of the dawn; and myself
Will lay myself straight in my bed,
And draw the sheet under my chin.

LANGOUR AFTER PAIN

Pain ebbs,
And like cool balm,
An opiate weariness,
Settles on eye-lids, on relaxed
Pale wrists.

THE GUARDED WOUND

If it
Were lighter touch
Than petal of flower resting

On grass oh still too heavy it were,
Too heavy!

WINTER

The cold
With steely clutch
Grips all the land. . alack,
The little people in the hills
Will die!

ON SEEING WEATHER-BEATEN TREES

Is it as plainly in our living shown,
By slant and twist, which way the wind hath blown?

LINES ADDRESSED TO MY LEFT LUNG
INCONVENIENTLY ENAMOURED OF PLANT-LIFE

It was, my lung, most strange of you,
    A freak I cannot pardon,
Thus to transform yourself into
    A vegetable-garden.

Though laking William set erewhile
    His seal on rural fashions,

I must deplore, bewail, revile
    Your horticultural passions.

And as your ways I thus lament
    (Which, plainly, I call crazy)
For all I know, serene, content,
    You think yourself a daisy!

LAMENT

Oh dear me, a maid unlucky,
Though I've searched the green fields over,
Peering, peeping, I have never
Found a single four-leaf clover.
Oh dear me, it's *most* unlucky.

MADNESS

Burdock,
Blue aconite,
And thistle and thorn. . of these,
Singing I wreathe my pretty wreath
O'death.

THE WARNING

Just now,
Out of the strange

Still dusk. . as strange, as still.
A white moth flew. Why am I grown
so cold?

THE ENTOMBMENT

In a cave born,
(Mary said)
In a cave is
My Son buried.

AUTUMN

Fugitive, wistful,
Pausing at edge of her going,
Autumn, the maiden, turns,
Leans to the earth with ineffable
Gesture. Ah, more than
Spring's skies her skies shine
Tender and frailer
Bloom than plum-bloom or almond
Lies on her hillsides, her fields,
Misted, faint-flushing. Ah, lovelier
Is her refusal than
Yielding who pauses with grave
Backward smiling, with light
Unforgettable touch of
Fingers withdrawn . . . Pauses, lo
Vanishes. . fugitive, wistful . . .

NOVEMBER NIGHT

Listen. .
With faint dry sound,
Like steps of passing ghosts,
The leaves, frost-crisp'd, break from the trees
And fall.

RELEASE

With swift
Great sweep of her
Magnificent arm my pain
Clanged back the doors that shut my soul
From life.

TRIAD

These be
Three silent things:
The falling snow. . the hour
Before the dawn. . the mouth of one
Just dead.

SNOW

Look up. . .
From bleakening hills
Blows down the light, first breath
Of wintry wind. . .look up, and scent
The snow!

FATE DEFIED

As it
Were tissue of silver
I'll wear, O Fate, thy grey,
And go mistily radiant, clad
Like the moon.

SONG

I make my shroud but no one knows,
So shimmering fine it is and fair,
With stitches set in even rows.
I make my shroud but no one knows.

In door-way where the lilac blows,
Humming a little wandering air,
I make my shroud and no one knows,
So shimmering fine it is and fair.

EVIL

In place secluded from the skies
A silent woman with strange eyes
Hiddenly waiting sits alone
Upon a royal-massive throne
Of smoothly polished malachite;
An emeraldine curious light
Fills all the place and through its chill
Sapphired pale glow, arrested still,
Unpalpitant as heart of death,
I watch her soft-drawn patient breath. . .

I will go creeping softly in
Her eyes are promises of sin.

Anne LaBastille

Anne LaBastille

Anne LaBastille found her way to the Adirondacks by chance; once there, she knew she had happened on the place where she could discover the woman she had always wanted to be — a woodswoman. Born in New York City and raised in suburban Montclair, New Jersey, she was the only child of a strong-willed mother who was a concert pianist and a distant father who was a professor of language. Early on, Anne's mother tried to quell the girl's inborn interest in the outdoors and her innate need for independence and self-reliance. When Anne asked for hiking boots and a rifle one Christmas, she was given instead nylon stockings and a dictionary. She was not permitted to learn to drive a car until she was nineteen years old. She was encouraged to study ballet and visit art shows and museums. Her experience of nature was limited to Girl Scout and Camp Fire Girl activities, romps with her dog on the local golf course, and idyllic summers at a lake in northern New Jersey. Books, especially *The Yearling*, carried her to back-country adventures.

When she was a teenager she blindly took a job at an Adirondack resort, and her interest in wilderness and wildlife began to grow from a vague passion to what is now a centered, fiercely protective love. From that first summer as a stable girl, she has evolved into an Adirondack guide and award-winning international wildlife consultant as well as an accomplished writer. Choosing to be a woodswoman was a rebellion which caused the rupture of the family relation. Her mother's civilizing influences on Anne included the gift of writing; her father gave her a love of travel and the athletic ability that invigorates her tiny frame. After her summer work at the Adirondack resort, she began undergraduate work at Cornell University where she completed a B.S. degree in wildlife conservation. Later, married to the resort's owner, she studied for her M.S. from Colorado State. After her divorce, she received her doctorate from Cornell University. She also holds an honorary doctorate from Union College as well as many other honors, awards and citations.

LaBastille is clear about what the mountain wilderness does for women. It provides a place where they can move about safely without fear of physical violence against them: no rape, murder and muggings threaten a woman in the wild. It is also a theater where they may test new skills, roles, and strengths. Back country is financially accessible to women, not bound by bureaucratic requirements like licenses, fees, and taxes. Yet she acknowledges that she might live in any wild area; it doesn't have to be the Adirondacks. They are simply the place she loves best on earth. The Adirondacks provide a delicious mix of creatures, trees, lakes and mountains in which she finds "a clear sense of the vital force at work in our ecosystems."[1] Whereas other women artists have shared their mountains through their works, LaBastille has taken this impulse to the personal level; she leads wilderness workshops, some especially for women, to open her beloved landscape to others. This accessibility is part of the allure of the wild. Natural spaces permit women to function on natural laws, to dress, walk, say what they will—wilderness becomes synonymous with freedom. And in the wild people learn to depend on each other, to see a man or woman as a person, not with gender but with capabilities.

The mountains offer LaBastille a testing ground, just as they do Alice Gilborn and Jean Rikhoff. There is terror in confronting a landscape that is not hostile but simply indifferent to human presence. The first selection which follows describes her night on Algonquin Mountain, an interesting parallel piece to Reben's account of her summit experience also included in this collection. In it, LaBastille shows the deliberate balance that represents her life in the wild. In *Women and Wilderness* she notes that wilderness allows one to keep inventory of oneself, providing a space in which—protected by the fact of isolation—one can turn inward. That book, published in 1980, explores the lives and careers of fifteen contemporary women who work in wilderness areas and gives a thoughtful overview of several wilderness women in American history. The author also recounts her own struggle with discrimination against women and her self-determination in becoming a professional woodswoman. Several of the women in LaBastille's study notice that men often pit themselves *against* nature while women more often work *with* it. Working against, into, and ultimately in accord with wild forces can give one great respect for the precision and efficiency of nature left alone. As LaBastille sees

it, "There's nothing romantic or sensuous about nature. It's the law!
. . . There's nothing moral or compassionate about the universe. It's
the law!"[2]

Although she shuns the romantic writer's view of nature,
LaBastille melds a poet's sensibility and insight with a scientist's
tough-minded vision. The result is a mix of fact and interpretation
wedded to her own almost deistic appreciation of the wild. An accomplished writer in many forms including scientific discourse, personal
narrative, and informal essay, she was established already as a conservation writer when an editor at Dutton suggested she write the book
that became her first, *Woodswoman*, published in 1976. Recovering
from a broken pelvis and unable to go out on her usual backpacking
and consulting jobs to earn her living as she had been doing since her
divorce, she received an advance of $5,000 to draft the book (which
was enough to support her through an Adirondack winter). With her
academic background and scientific training, it seems curious that she
has developed a style that is so consciously literary. Many of the images she employs are domestic, a use of figures that makes the
unknown wilderness less threatening by bringing it within the human
— especially the female — domain. In *Woodswoman* she narrates the
drama of finding herself at last in an environment where she could be
the pioneer she believed was within her. It is a story of discovery of
the wilderness as well as of the woman.

Assignment Wildlife appeared two years later and is equally in-
timate as a portrait of a professional woman conservationist making
her way in alien territories. In it she details her adventures in wilderness areas in Guatemala where she was largely responsible for the
salvation of the giant grebe, an achievement for which she received
the World Wildlife Fund Gold Medal in 1974. Her efforts on behalf
of animals are more global than personal, in contrast to those of Martha
Reben, for example. Even when LaBastille adopted two injured
quetzel chicks, it was not for mothering but for science — to be able to
photograph and study them. That is typical of her connection to the
land: living in harmony, not meddling with natural processes any
more than absolutely necessary, maintaining one's part in the web of
being.

That harmony is carefully nurtured by LaBastille when she is at
home at her cabin "West of the Wind." Like Thoreau, she built herself a dwelling-place for the soul, a place that by its very creation

declared independence. However, the popularity of *Woodswoman* and increased traffic on the lakes in the Adirondacks has eroded the peace of Black Bear Lake. As a result, the writer has built a retreat deeper in the woods, "Thoreau II." It is the building of this second cabin that provides the structure for her most recent book *Beyond Black Bear Lake*. The theme of building for independence and solitude recurs in this newest work about her second decade as a woodswoman and the painstaking construction of this second, smaller cabin on a remote pond. Thoreau's *Walden* informs this book. LaBastille writes carefully and conscientiously of her decision to go deeper into the wild and — using Thoreau's narrative as a model — explores the economy and philosophy that emerged in the going. This is a very different work from *Woodswoman*. The writer's transcendental consciousness is more fully realized. She now sees even more clearly the inner and outer landscapes; as a result this book is both more thoughtful and thought-provoking. She looks hard at how we live with the land, comparing that to how our nineteenth century forebears did, and finds that we are not doing enough of the right things. *Beyond Black Bear Lake* is both a place on the map and an attitude toward salvaging the land.

The more deeply LaBastille has travelled in wilderness areas and among unschooled people, the more she has learned of the "the occult, the extrasensory side of life."[3] This mysticism runs as an undercurrent through her prose, but hers is not a spiritual quest which leads her to a certified religion. She is by her own definition, "a-religious," self-reliant in spritual matters. What she has come to believe in is a great power which regulates human lives, a power which is partially revealed in things like sun signs and non-traditional methods of healing, which she suspects have scientific bases awaiting sophisticated research. For LaBastille, mysticism and science merge. In the chapter, "Among My Closest Friends" from *Woodswoman*, included here, this mingling of seemingly opposed attitudes emerges with elegant unity. At the end of that book, when she returns to her mountain home from a stint in Washington, D.C., her connection to that transcendant principle infuses her:

> I'm gradually imbued with the ordered goodness of our earth. Its gentle, implacable push toward balance, regularity, homeostasis. This seeps into

my soul as surely as spagnum moss absorbs water. Surely the entire universe must be operating in this way.[4]

For her, this union is eternal, part of the essential cycle. When she dies, the writer wants her ashes strewn beneath her pines, the same ones she numbers among her closest friends: "my energy and body will enter the earth . . . to be recycled into new forms of life."[5] She speaks of the mountains in religious terms; when she cuts trees for her dwellings she offers silent prayers to thank them and ask that her days at Thoreau II be "safe, serene, and inspiring."[6] She notes that her retreat looks like a shrine; she writes lovingly and reverently of nameless forest gods and of the mountain wilderness hushed like a cathedral:

> I felt as though I was sitting at the very core of something . . . . I could plainly "feel" them, their "*Gestalt*," their ancientness, solidarity, reliability. They were very comfortable mountains, deep-rooted, well-preserved. They were not given to sudden outbursts of lava flows, landslides, earthquakes, hurricanes, floods, droughts, or erosion. It was like living with a grandparent who could always be counted on.[7]

The mountains have become the ultimate generative force, the "grand" parent as well as the perfect home for this writer. In a human world of transcience and riot, the Adirondacks endure.

We parted company shortly afterward; he to detour up Wright's Peak, and I to climb right up Algonquin. I reached the summit by late afternoon. The sky was entirely clear and faultlessly blue. The view was far better than on Marcy. I could look one way across ranges of purple mountains towards the gentler hills of the western Adirondacks. Turning half a circle, I gazed down to Lake Champlain and its lowlands before lifting my eyes again to the lavender outline of Vermont's Green Mountains. South, I thought I detected the smudge of smog which would be Albany and Hudson River valley towns 100 miles way.

The setting sun was throwing an intense glow over the entire mountain-top while the clefts below were darkening with shadows. I began looking for a camping spot, determined to stay right at the top overnight to absorb the beauty of sunset and sunrise. Skirting around gigantic boulders, mounds of bedrock, and clusters of alpine flowers and miniature trees, I tried not to destroy anything. Finally I found a flat patch of moss, lichens, and a creeping shrub which looked large enough to accommodate my tent and offer some cushioning. The guy lines and corners had to be held taut with rocks because the soil was too shallow to hold tent pegs. Here and there pockets in the bedrock held pools of rain water. Enough for Pitzi and me to cook with and drink.

My tent flaps faced west into a glorious sunset. As the swollen sun lowered, its rays turned my tent into a translucent scarlet balloon, my pack into a burnished copper-orange sack. The small campfire flickered with hot orange flames. Now the sun sat on the jagged edge of purple-black mountains. The world was orange and purple for a moment, before the sun was swallowed. I took a last look around the horizon. Never before had I sensed so keenly the immensity, grandeur, and wildness of these mountains. As an early guide remarked, "It makes a man feel what it is to have all creation under his feet."

Suddenly it was twilight and a chill crept into the air. Not a breath of wind. Far off to the south, practically on the rim of the sky, a few thin skeins of cloud turned rosy. A lone jet trail overhead flared crimson for a minute, then turned ghostly gray. I pulled on a down jacket and traded hiking shorts for jeans. Pitzi was already curled up asleep in a little hollow. Yet I stayed up until it was totally dark and watched the night cross the sky and the stars break out in spangles. Not a sound broke the alpine stillness—no planes, no cars, no animals, no trees, no people, no running water. It was an exceptional night on top of the High Peaks, probably 1 out of 300.

Toward dawn, my tent began to flap and quiver in a strange manner. I half woke, listening for wind, imagining how easily one could be blown off this precipitous mountaintop in a gale. I could detect no gusts, so I fell asleep again.

A glance out the tent at dawn showed me why the tent had quivered and the predicament I was in. A front had moved up from the innocent-looking south. I should have paid attention to the smudgelike smog and the wispy cloud strands. A wall of fog and mist was rolling over the mountaintops, descending from the sky, obscuring everything. I crawled out, stood up, and saw a monstrously inflamed red ball poised on the horizon, silhouetting two stunted spruces, no higher than my knee, and probably 150 years old. Then abruptly, the sunrise was snuffed out. Fingers of fog closed over the top of Algonquin like a giant hand enclosing a giant breast. I could see no farther than 50 feet.

Working swiftly, I struck the tent, repacked, saddled the dog with his bags, stamped out the fire remains, and swallowed half a cup of stale cold tea. All the while I kept peering into the gloom, hoping for a break. I began to feel disoriented. I could no longer remember where the first cairn lay which marked the way off the rocky summit. I could find no trace of footsteps or scuffmarks on the smooth stones around me. With a compass, of course, I could always strike out in the general direction I had climbed up from, but if I missed the trail at timberline, the dog and I might spend hours struggling through stunted firs and birches before reaching the more open, taller forests below.

Pitzi and I began our first tentative steps down the summit. The murk swirled about us. I had rapidly learned a new lesson in backpacking and camping: Never camp above timberline! Weather can change dramatically in the Adirondacks. Extremes of temperature and wind are common atop the High Peaks. With luck and an occasional glimpse through the fog, we made it safely down the mountain; and a short time later, safely off the Northville-Lake Placid Trail.

∽❧∾

AMONG MY CLOSEST FRIENDS

During those first weeks and months at the cabin my close and constant companions were trees. I became intimately acquainted with every tree inside a 400-foot radius. What at first seemed like a dense stand of random temperate-zone vegetation—maples, spruces, hemlocks, beeches, birches, and pines—gradually introduced itself as an orderly congregation of unique individuals.

The "Four Sisters," a neatly spaced row of red spruces, stood practically within spitting distance of my sleeping loft. A trio of the same species clustered behind and above the dock, acting as friendly navigational aids against night skies. An enormous white pine leaned above the outhouse and another rose straight as a lighthouse on the point near the rocks. A forest of young firs graced the high shoreline from the side of the cabin almost down to the creek. Five more prodigious spruces loomed from a wet pocket of ground beyond the woodshed, while under them a few spindly youngsters stretched for the sun. I came to touch them all through trimming, pruning, clearing, cutting, admiring, and listening.

The first trees I got to know, and later draw strength from, were the mature, towering red spruces and white pines. These were highly skilled veterans, seasoned in survival techniques. They had started fortuitously as seedlings upon rich, sun-dappled patches of earth. They had escaped being nibbled by snowshoe hares, mice, grouse, or deer. They had shouldered past their siblings and finally pushed above the forest canopy into the free blue sky where swallows wheeled in summer and snowflakes whirled in winter. Here *all* the sunlight on any given day was theirs to activate the chlorophyll-laden needles, and *all* the rain of any given storm was theirs to wash the thick branches. These trees had survived attacks of smuts, aphids, mites, molds, beetles, galls, caterpillars, viruses, and the other miniature, life-robbing enemies of the plant world. They had also escaped being scratched by falling limbs, ripped by bears' claws, chafed by trunks, or rubbed by deer antlers. Likewise they had been unscathed by forest fires and bypassed by hurricanes. And so, in 1964, a goodly 300 years after their germination, they towered as invincible individuals of great character, lending dignity and beauty to my land.

I developed an amazing awareness of these trees. First, I noticed their noises. In wind, the spruces gave off a somber, deep sad whoosh, while the pines made a higher, happier softer sound. After my initial surprise at the differences in sound between these two species, I began listening to other kinds of trees. Balsam firs made a short, precise, polite swishing, red and sugar maples gave an impatient rustling; yellow birches, a gentle, restful sighing.

Of course, these strains of sound can be explained by the size, shape, flexibility, and thickness of leaf or needle. They can also be explained by the wind itself. I noticed distinct variations produced by the fresh westerly breezes, fierce north fronts, petulant south zephyrs, or stormy east winds. But the sound of the forest is more than this—just as a symphony is more than the sizes and shapes of the instruments, air pressure or touch which activate them to make music, and the players.

Next I discovered a whole assortment of tree scents. On hot, dry summer days, the balsams, spruces, and pines acted like giant sticks of incense, giving off a redolence which filled the air inside and outside the cabin. The carpet of dead needles, the dry duff, the trickles of pitch, the sun-warmed bark itself, all gave off subtle odors. The live needles tanged the air with what old-time doctors called "balsamifers."

The presence of this restorative odor is what made the Adirondacks a mecca for tubercular patients in the late 1800s and early 1900s. Whether the "balsamifers" did the curing, or the clean cold air, the long rests, the inspiring views, and the presence of such medical prophets as Dr. E. L. Trudeau, many mortally sick patients recovered in the Adirondacks. I know three men, all in their spry eighties, who came here to die in their thirties. They believe, as did Trudeau, pioneer tuberculosis researcher, that the resinous aromas produced by the evergreen forests helped cure them. Recent scientific studies have, in fact, revealed that the turpentine vapor exuded by conifers has a purifying effect on the local atmosphere and plays a part in keeping Adirondack air remarkably pure and healthy.

Another beautiful sensory experience happened to me in my forest of young balsam firs. On late summer afternoons, I saw the sun come slanting between the trunks. The light gave a glorious golden glow to the dense, dark copse. I began trimming off dead branches as high as I could reach with an axe. Whenever I nicked the bark of a trunk, I'd carefully daub moist earth on the wound to lessen sap flow and prevent the entry of disease organisms or insects. Off and on all summer I trimmed the balsam boles farther and farther away from the cabin until I achieved the desired effect. Then on a still September evening I perched on the porch railing, picking pitch from my palms, and watched the setting sum illuminate my fir forest. The sun shafts were straight diagonals of gold-washed air. As far as I could see, the balsam boles were straight black bars which threw black shadows onto the burnished-copper ground, golden-green moss, and bronzed fallen logs. My little forest had become a study in light and shadow, a stained glass window of gold and green panes with black bars, back-lit by the setting sun.

I experienced another quality of light on a dismal, dripping November day. It had rained for a week and the forest was totally drenched. My giant spruce trunks were soaked to charcoal-gray, their branches grizzly-green, the balsam boles inky black, the ground tarry-brown, the pines pewter-gray. As Thomas Hardy wrote, "The whole world dripped in browns and duns." About eleven o'clock in the morning, the quality of light surrounding the cabin and trees was so watery that I might have been submerged somewhere in the North Atlantic. Each gust of rain felt like the surge of a swell, and the soggy forest looked like a stand of seaweed.

As I became more tuned into trees, I began to admire the enormous white pine near the path to the outhouse. I even oriented the entrance of the outhouse so that I could gaze at this tall, furrowed tree while sitting there. It was much better than reading *Time* magazine. In strong winds, the trunk would sway in a sinuous motion which combined the suppleness of a snake with the strength of an elephant. No rigidity to that pine. The thick bark, its multiple rings of the wood, the very heart of the trunk all moved with a fluidity more animallike than plant. I drew closer to the tree and eventually came to stand against the trunk in order to watch those tons of wood bending lithely above my head. The grace and rhythm almost hypnotized me.

These friendly discoveries about my trees and the companionship which has been growing between us for years do not prevent me from using them at times for survival purposes. In a very practical way, trees have played an important role in my adult life, at times even a dangerous one.

Before I built my house from the bodies of trees, I used to help my husband, Morgan, cut wood for the hotel. We needed to put up at least 40 cords of firewood a year, besides bringing enough logs to the sawmill to provide lumber for the basic repairs and additions to our buildings. With fourteen fireplaces to feed, eight cottages, a large main house, garages, stables, docks, and boardwalks to maintain, we had to cut a lot of timber each fall. And so I became a lumberjack, even being carried on the hotel payroll as such.

Coming from a populous suburb of New York City, I had never wielded an axe, revved up a chain saw, pulled a crosscut, or driven a wedge. After my first fall in the Adirondacks, however, I was able to cut and split 10 of those 40 cords, run a power saw, and operate the winch truck. I loved being a lumberjack, or "timberbeast." After a big breakfast, Morgan and I pulled on our steel-shanked and -toed boots, grabbed heavy duty leather work gloves, and drove two trucks back into the woods over old logging roads. One truck had an iron A-frame which supported a pulley and winch cable for lifting logs; the other had a flatbed for transporting them. Locating an area of straight, tall hardwoods, we would pick a tree. Usually Morgan would start the chain saw and begin the cut while I stood back and watched the top. When the tree began to quiver, I would give hand signals which warned Morgan to stop the saw and dash away from the butt. He had to be careful that the severed trunk would not pinch down on the saw blade, kick back, or splinter as it fell. Then we both held our breaths and stood until the tree struck the earth with an awesome crash.

Once the tree was down, I usually darted up the trunk to the first limbs and began lopping them off with an axe. I worked upward until the trunk was too knotty or small to produce good firewood or lumber. Meanwhile, Morgan was busy sawing off the lower section into 8-foot, 12-foot, or 16-foot lengths which would be loaded onto the log truck. Later, at the hotel these would be blocked off into 18-inch sections for splitting, or taken directly to the sawmill for rough lumber, planking, and slab siding.

Switching off the ear-shattering saw and removing our ear-protector headsets, each of us started a truck. The winch truck was driven as close to the logs as possible and the flatbed backed up beside it. I would loosen the winch drum, drag the 3/8-inch steel cable out to the log, wrap and hook it around the butt end. Morgan would operate the controls from the cab of the winch truck. As soon as I made sure that the cable was running smoothly up to and through the pulley, I'd jerk my thumb upward in the signal, "All ready, lift up."

Morgan would start the cable winding on the drum and the log would be snaked through the woods. Once it was near the flatbed, Morgan slacked off the cable and I unhooked it from the log. Now a pair of heavy iron log tongs was hung on the cable hook, and I placed these at the center of the log.

Thumb up, I'd watch the 1,000-pound monster rise (hoping nothing would break just then) above my head. A shove this way or that aligned the log with the flatbed of the other truck. When it hung just right, I'd jerk my thumb down, "Let down." Morgan would lower the log by unwinding the cable. I hopped up on the flatbed and unhooked the tongs. A couple of chocks under the log assured me it wouldn't roll on my foot by mistake. Now we were ready to drag in another log, but before that, I had time to play a little game. In fact, it was the reason I preferred this half of the loading stint. Placing each boot inside the hooks of the tongs and grabbing the steel cable with my gloved hands, I would "ride" down from the truck bed to the ground, swinging like a monkey on a vine, as Morgan slowly let out the cable.

One morning, with six logs already on the flatbed, I was about to indulge in my usual pastime. As I grabbed the cable just below the pulley, my husband shifted the gears into "lift up" instead of "let down" by mistake. Before I realized what was happening, my glove and index finger were being ground up with the cable into the pulley. I let out a terrific scream. Morgan was so startled that he jammed in the brake, stalled the engine, and left me hanging. Continued screeching galvanized him into action. Seconds later the engine was running and I was descending to the ground. The shock of picturing myself being wound implacably through the winch like a mangled strip of hamburger almost made me pass out. I was afraid to pull off the glove. Morgan rushed me to a stream, dashed handfuls of icy water in my face, and plunged my right hand into the water. As it numbed from the cold, he gently eased off the glove. It was impossible to tell if bones were broken or tendons severed in the bloody wound.

The log truck was too heavily laden to make time, so Morgan carried me to the winch truck and drove flat out down the logging road. We had to cover about 35 miles of rough dirt and paved roads to the nearest clinic and X-ray machine. I was lucky. None of my fingers were broken or rendered useless. A couple of weeks later I was logging again, only this time *I* ran the winch and let *Morgan* hook and handle the logs.

Logging *can* be dangerous; however, this was the only accident either of us ever sustained during several fall seasons of logging. I gradually grew more adept with a chain saw. I could cut branches over my head, release trees tightly wedged against other trees, sever logs pinched together with an underhand cut, saw out planks, and even do some simple carpentry. This training, of course, made the construction of my log cabin possible and far easier than I ever suspected.

In those early days at the hotel, we employed Stan, an old-time lumberjack cook, as our off-season chef. He became my good friend. We whiled away many hours, he preparing roasts, me baking cakes, both singing lumberjack songs.

Stan taught me a tremendous respect for the early Adirondack timber-beasts. He told me of the prodigious appetites of these legendary men who wolfed down a dozen eggs and a stack of pancakes as tall as their boots for breakfast. He explained their incredible need for calories—over 6,000 a day—to pull crosscut saws for hours, ride slippery logs downriver, clear limbs, split wood, load logs, and drive horses in twelve-hour shifts. Stan would laugh when I came in ravenous from splitting firewood to devour slabs of roast beef and two pieces of pie.

"You eat like a cocker spaniel," he chuckled, "and your guests eat like toy poodles. You should have seen the meals I used to prepare for those lumberjacks!"

Stan also reminisced on logging-camp life. There was usually a shanty lined with narrow bunk beds, a cookhouse, and dining area. Silence was enforced at meals, except for requests for second, third, and fourth helpings, so as to lessen the chance for arguments and brawls. At night, the men would tumble into squalid straw-filled bunks. Often they would have to pluck lice from their hair by day. There were no washing machines in camp; but periodically, the cook, man or woman, would boil up the lumberjack's clothes on a wood fire, thus removing some of the ingrained pitch, sweat, and soil. Timberbeasts worked all winter without a break (or a drink). They were without any transportation in or out except in emergencies. Then during a short spree in town, they might blow their entire earnings.

"God Almighty!" declared Stan. "What drinking sprees they used to go on. An 'Adirondack haircut'—that's what we called it. Some haircuts lasted three weeks!"

Logging hit the Adirondacks in the mid to late 1800's. Wave after wave of lumberjacks passed through. Most came from outside the mountains, from the farming valleys and river bottoms. They were French Canadians, Swedes, Germans, Irish, and Welsh. Timberbeasts cut and snaked logs out of the wood with enormous, clever, patient horses. Winter was the best time for hauling logs via sled because the logging roads could be watered down and immediately turned to ice. This made it easier for the powerful teams to pull heavy loads. Logs were piled beside the closest lake, river, canal, or creek. Come spring, they were dumped into the water which was running abnormally high from the runoff. Then nimble loggers with caulked shoes, pegged trousers, and pike piles, "drove" the logs downstream to sawmills or railroads.

"Many a man lost his life on those river drives," mourned Stan, thumping a mound of sourdough for biscuits. "Once he fell in that icy river water, he either drowned, got knocked on the noggin' with a log, or was smashed up in a log jam. Jams were the most dangerous of all." Then he added cheerfully, "Say, did you hear about the lumberjack who turned up his heels at

Tupper Lake last week? Clamps on his winch cable broke and a 1,200 pound log dropped on his head. Yes, indeedy, logging has always been dangerous work!"

Helping Stan stamp out biscuits with a cutter, I thought of all the logs that had lifted above *my* head back in the woods. A shudder ran through me. Then I considered that today's lumberjacks really *do* have a safer, easier existence. They are protected by NIOSH (the National Institute of Occupational Safety and Health), they normally live at home, commute to work, eat better food, and use remarkable new power tools. On top of that, they can do their fighting and drinking on weekends. Adirondack haircuts have gone out of style. So have lice.

The other thing that is going out of style is the "rape attitude" of earlier days. In the 1800s, opportunists literally ravished the Adirondack forests. A lumberman's credo was, "If it grows, cut it." Clear-cutting and timber stealing were rampant. New York State led all states in 1850 in volume of timber cut. Due to this attitude, the Adirondack forest was swiftly devastated. Great tracts were cut—first the high pines and spruces to make spars and spiles (masts for sailing ships and spiles for docks), then the smaller softwoods for lumber, next the hemlocks for the tannic acid in their bark, and finally the hardwoods to provide furniture, veneer, tool handles, and other wooden merchandise.

Wildfires burned thousands of acres more. Sparks from logging camps and steam locomotives fell upon tinder-dry piles of branches, bark, and cull logs. The ensuing fires might smolder in the rich organic soil or leap into the crowns, burning for weeks without any control. People noticed that Adirondack streams and rivers were becoming "every year more slender and fitful."

The Adirondacks needed to be saved. Slowly public opinion turned toward conservation and legislators began to fight. In 1885, the state Adirondack Forest Preserve was created. Then in 1894, the famous "forever wild" amendment (Article 14) was added to the Constitution in order to protect the timber and watersheds of the Forest Preserve.

This legal gem reads: "The lands of the State, now owned or hereafter acquired, constituting the forest preserve as fixed by law shall be forever kept as wild forest lands. They shall not be leased, sold or exchanged, or be taken by any corporation, public or private, nor shall the timber thereupon be sold or removed or destroyed."

This far-sighted, totally unprecedented, wise conservation act is actually what made my dream of building a cabin in the wilderness—in the second most-populated state in the Union—possible. Because of it, I have almost 3 million acres of untouched forest as my backyard. Without it, I shudder to think what scruffy piece of cutover land I might have purchased in my search for a home in the woods.

Today Adirondack trees still provide hundreds of thousands of board feet of lumber per year. Logging is our second most important industry up here, but it operates only on private holdings. Several large companies, such as International Paper, Litchfield Paper, and St. Regis Paper, employ lumberljacks. Timber is trucked to big mills outside the Adirondack Park. I often meet heavily loaded trucks bound for the Ticonderoga paper mill on the road to Hawk Hill. I always give them a wide berth, preferring to run off the shoulder and into a swamp than to match paints with a 20-ton truck whose stack of logs leans ominously over my small half-ton pickup.

Even though our Adirondack trees are protected from chain saws and axes on *state* land, they are still vulnerable everywhere to wind storms and lightning. In the great "blowdowns" of 1950 and 1954 trees toppled like pick-up sticks. Local events are still dated from these two most catastrophic hurricanes. On the eve of one less diasterous storm, I spent the entire night wandering through the woods. It was as warm as the tropics. That wild wind had blown up from Miami itself. High humidity soaked the air, swollen clouds gusted over the treetops, the air seemed spiced with scents from the Gulf of Mexico. I rolled up my shirtsleeves and stopped by a stream to splash sweat off my face. The branches above me roared and thrashed. From time to time tall timber cracked and crashed to the ground. For one moment a three-quarter moon poured its wan light into the woods as monstrous blue-black clouds rent apart. I was too exhilarated to feel afraid, too thrilled to feel tired. The winds diminished around 5 A.M. Only then did I go to bed, still oblivious to the danger I had foolheartedly courted.

I awoke to devastation. Some sections of the Adirondack forest had been leveled as if by a scythe. Trunks lay crisscrossed in places up to 20 feet above the ground. Some of the finest mature timber in the Northeast had gone down in that storm. Effects of blowdowns last for years. New forest reproduction allows deer to increase dramatically in some places, starve out in other areas where fallen trees severely hamper movement. The lumber companies lose heavily, although they attempt to draw out whatever timber can be salvaged before decay spoils the wood. Hikers and campers find trails and campsites destroyed or blocked. Fire crews face new hazards as downed trees die and dry out.

It seems curious that I was not at all frightened *then* to be walking in the forest during those high winds, while *today* I am filled with apprehension about falling trees. It runs a close second to my preoccupation with fire. However, I've taken a deliberate gamble. Esthetically, it is more essential to me to see the Four Sisters swaying against the stars on a windy night than to cut a safety space all around the cabin. It is more important to have the huge curved spruce artistically jutting out from under my sun deck than to fell it and clear out a nice secure lawn instead. Despite the decision, I still don't sleep well on nights when the wind is high. I picture a great trunk toppling against a wall and scattering books, logs, and chinking into every corner. I lie awake imagining a great mass of branches plummeting onto my ridgepole, poking through the metal sheets and roof boards, and impaling me in bed.

Only once have I had a close call. An exceptionally strong winter cold front swept through from the north and snapped the living top off my splendid curved spruce. It was blown 20 feet through the air. It sailed over the cabin ridge, slid down the back side, and crashed to earth with just its 15-inch butt nuding into the edge of the woodshed roof. Even this close call has not changed my decision to gamble, nor my original vow to protect the trees. I still cut only those which are dead.

In getting to know my trees, an exceptional event occurred. On my trips back and forth to the outhouse, I took more and more enjoyment from touching the great white pine. One morning, with my arms wrapped around the trunk, I began to feel a sense of peace and well-being. I held on for over fifteen minutes, chasing extraneous thoughts from my mind. The rough bark was pressed hard against my skin. It was as though the tree was pouring its life-force into my body. When I stepped away from the white pine, I had the definite feeling that we had exchanged some form of life energy. This feeling seemed concentrated between my belly and breasts. In later readings, I found the explanation in Carlos Casteneda's *Conversations with Don Juan* and Michael Serano's *Serpent of Serpico*. Mention is made that the area of the navel and solar plexus is considered the main point of energy in the human body. From here, "fibers" or "rays" of life-force radiate. I have also seen the energy coronas around fingertips in Kerlian photography and the results registered by polygraphs hooked up to plants reacting to stimuli. All these phenomena point to the presence of a pervading life-force, one which I miraculously tuned into by getting to know the trees at my cabin.

I feel this communion, this strange attunement, most readily with large white pines, a little less with big spruces, sugar maples, beeches, or oaks. Clearly white pines and I are on the same wavelength. What I give back to the trees I cannot imagine. I hope they receive something, because trees are among my closest friends.

∾❀∽

A COPYCAT WALDEN

The heart of a cabin in the woods is its stove or fireplace. Its fire is the heartbeat, the life throb, which makes existence possible in these cold climes. Thoreau managed with a brick fireplace in his cabin, whereas I use an old potbellied stove in mine.

Mary gave me the stove when she moved. It was part cast iron, part steel, stood about four feet high, and weighed close to sixty pounds. The only way I could get it to Lilypad Lake was to wait till winter and toboggan it up through the snowy woods and over the ice-covered pond. This worked well. I left the stove smothered in plastic bags standing against a big spruce. A year and a half later, when I was ready to install the stove inside the cabin, it was intact, though somewhat rusty. One leg had cracked and would not support the stove's weight. Rod solved the problem by giving me four old firebricks to prop beneath. Snuggled in the bottom of my pack basket, they weighed thirty-two pounds. He hiked in with me to set the stove damper into a section of pipe and put the whole rig together. Installing stove pipes, like laying up rafters, is one of those cabin chores which demand two people to make it a success. Rod shoved the pipes through the hole in the wall and up in the air. We pushed on either side of the pipes until they were firmly together and the elbows on. I attached the cap and wired it securely to the cabin roof. We then nailed a sheet of asbestos against the inner wall to prevent possible fire.

It was time to try the stove out. Rod brought in some yellow birch bark curls and dry spruce branches, laid the fire, opened the damper, and struck a match. Within minutes a toasty warmth was radiating through the cabin while those shiny new stove pipes turned ashen gray in color as they "cured" from the heat. Everything worked fine, with a good draft. I dashed outside to see smoke rising above the roof and felt in my heart a glow as warm as the stove. Thoreau II was alive! And I could live there any time I wanted to.

In planning my furnishings, I decided to copy Thoreau's cottage at Walden Pond as far as was practical. My resolve was to take only essentials to the cabin, and certainly Thoreau was a master of economy. I made a list of the furniture and utensils he'd used and his general floor plan.

To begin with, the Walden cabin measured ten feet by fifteen feet, had a door, two windows, a closet, and a garret. There was a six-by-six-by-seven-foot root cellar for food storage. In contrast, Thoreau II was ten feet by ten feet, had two doors (screen and outer), two windows (main floor and loft), nails for hanging clothing, and a tiny loft. Instead of a root cellar, I carried in a large box of freeze-dried foods and other dry staples. I didn't want the slightest odor or taint of stored food to attract bears or raccoons. Both could ransack a place, but bears were positively destructive. If they caught the scent of something to eat, they usually broke into and entered a camp one way and exited another way, leaving large holes in the windows or doors. I'm not sure if black bears lived around Walden Pond in Massachusetts in the mid-1800s or if Thoreau faced a similar problem, but I felt justified in calling on this technological improvement over a root cellar.

As furniture and utensils, Thoreau included a bed, a table, a desk, three chairs, a looking glass three inches in diameter, a pair of tongs and andirons, a kettle, skillet, and frying pan, a dipper and washbowl, two knives and forks, three plates, one cup, one jug for oil, one for molasses, and a japanned (old-fashioned oil) lamp.

I deviated from Thoreau's plan by using a loft rather than a bed for sleeping, having my desk do double duty as an eating table, and using a stove rather than a fireplace with its attendant tools. Finally I treated myself to a *four*-inch mirror. I also carried in *three* knives, forks, spoons, and cups (why else have *three* plates?), a shiny metal pail for water, an old dipper, and kerosene in a plastic bottle. My only new purchases were a pail made in Mexico (cost: $2.89) and a pretty green glass kerosene lamp. There was no crockery jug for molasses, but there was a tin can with maple syrup.

Modern utensils not mentioned by the earlier woods dweller were a can opener, several cans of dog food, two dog dishes, two empty Grizzly Bear beer bottles and two Black Tower wine bottles for candleholders, and, of course, candles.

Thoreau had three chairs—"one for solitude, two for friendship, and three for society." That became my rule of thumb as well.

Two of my chairs were old dark oak folding types—from the pew of an abandoned chapel—which slipped under the desk. The third was a slender rocker set beside the stove. Thoreau also mentioned having paper, pens, books, and matches in Walden as well as a coffee mill. I had all the former, plus a typewriter, which I had purchased for $2.50 at the Salvation Army outlet store and carried in via a pack basket. I had no need for a coffee mill because my cabin was well stocked with cans of redolent Cuban espresso coffee obtained in Miami.

Other than his washbowl, Thoreau never discussed cleanliness in his book. Perhaps he was a dirty old bird with soiled underpants and cavities in his teeth. For my part, I've never felt comfortable being unkempt in the woods or in my cabin. So I brought an extensive list of items in this department. Besides the four-inch mirror, I had a comb, toothbrush, toothpaste, toilet paper, soap, skin cream and towels. There was my old standby, the round horse-drinking tub which I used to bathe in outdoors on the porch during winter months at West of the Wind. I would fill it with buckets of hot water, scrunch myself in, cover my shoulders and head with a big poncho, and let the steam envelop me. Even when snow was falling, I kept warm and got clean. A broom, whisk broom, liquid detergent, scouring pads, and dish mop completed the household cleansing inventory.

Another subject Thoreau never addressed was safety. He must have had the eyes of a lynx and the luck of an Irishman the way he wandered through the woods at night without any form of light. Some of his descriptions of returning home from town during storms are downright scary! I made sure to have flashlights and batteries in case of an emergency evacuation at night; a small transistor radio with batteries so I could hear weather reports; some first-aid gear, pain-killers, and an Ace bandage. Another safety measure was heavy wire nailed over the windows in the autumn to discourage bears and hunters from breaking in.

Perhaps the greatest difference between Thoreau and me in furnishing our cabins lay in the realm of aesthetics. While I was content to use nails as hooks for clothes and towels, rip planks out of logs for shelving, and attach an old wooden thread spool to the door as a handle, I did not intend to live without curtains, a rug, some bright cushions, colored candles, and a poster or two on the walls. The rug caused the whole room to blend with the outdoors. The design was called Stained Glass, a patchwork of muted greens, beiges, browns, and rusts separated by black lines. When I looked at it, I thought of spruce branches in silhouette against the lake and hills at twilight.

Friends marveled that I could live and function in a ten-foot-by-ten-foot building. But basically there was room for everything, and the room was streamlined. The narrow plywood desk (six feet by two feet) ran under the front windows with a beautiful view of Lilypad. It was the desk I had had since I began free-lancing twenty years before. The two chapel chairs slipped underneath the desk or folded against the wall. The sink I'd transported from Miami sat in one corner with the Mexican pail in the tub part and a two-burner gas Coleman stove on the flat section. (I wasn't going to cook on a campfire in sleet and snow.) Moreover, the sink was a lovely avocado color which matched the rug. The rocker took up the center of the room and was covered with a cherished old Kentucky patchwork quilt. The potbellied stove stood against the north wall between rocker and desk with a woodpile beside it. (That being the coldest wall, it was the best place for the stove.) High shelves held numerous odds and ends. Since the cabin walls were seven feet high, I did not feel jammed in or overhung with gear.

The sleeping loft held two foam rubber pads (retired from my camping equipment), which ran the length of the windows, end to end. There were two sleeping bags, two pillows, and two red and white blankets. Red candles in the Black Tower bottles lent a cheerful touch and were sufficient for reading. Ricky and Linda's makeshift ladder gave access to the loft, provided one was part red squirrel.

My outhouse (something else Thoreau failed to mention in *Walden*) was made from three old long French doors, which a neighbor had given me years before. Through the glass panes on the upper part, I could gaze out at the forest, while the solid wooden lower section provided privacy. I used them as three sides of the building, with a gigantic yellow birch tree trunk as the fourth side and partial roof. I dug a hole deep among its roots, figuring that the wastes might act as fertilizer to the tree. Over the hole I set the plastic toilet housing I'd found in a deer hunter's camp. As at West of the Wind's outhouse, I used ashes from the stove to purify and deodorize excrement.

As the cabin neared completion in September, I began listing all the expenses and comparing them to what Thoreau had spent for his place 140 years before. Our purchases look like this: Thoreau spent $30.12 2/2; I spent $130.75, total.

Since we *both* used the free trees on our properties for the wood, probably the two biggest expenses for *both* of us were nails and spikes for building and stove or fireplace materials for warmth and cooking. There is just no other way to obtain metal materials such as stovepipes, damper, spikes, and so forth other than having a sheet metal worker or blacksmith as your good pal. And neither of these departments is a good place to skimp, for you don't want your cabin to fall down or burn up.

The other noteworthy difference in costs involved the state tax, the town building permit, and correspondence over Adirondack Park Agency regulations. None of these had existed in Thoreau's day. With what I paid out in state taxes for my purchases ($7.77), *he* was able to build his brick fireplace! *My* local building permit cost more than all *his* boards. And although an APA permit was not necessary, I spent as much in postage back and forth as Thoreau spent in oil for eight months. So much for bureaucracy!

Finally, and sadly, there was my need for a hasp and padlock. Not too long ago in the Adirondacks (and, of course, in Thoreau's time), people could leave their camps unlocked, pack baskets standing in the woods, boats overturned on wild lakeshores. No one would enter or steal or damage anything. Today the threat of thievery and meddling from a few nasty hunters, hikers, or fishermen or from thoughtless teenagers makes it so that no one dares leave a house or boat unlocked, a backpack or pack basket unattended.

When I clicked shut the lock on the cabin door, I felt both safer and more nostalgic. The time for trusting one's fellow human being is fast passing. Thoreau wrote about finding visitors who had come in to his cabin and left their cards, "either a bunch of flowers, or a wreath of evergreen, or a name in pencil on a yellow walnut leaf or a chip." People were free to come and go. He never locked his door, even come evening. ". . . the black kernel of the night was never profaned by any human neighborhood." People invariably left "the world to darkness and to me."

I'm sure if I left *my* door open, half my gear would disappear during hunting season. At night I *always* lock the door, even with two German shepherds to guard me and a pistol under my pillow.

Whereas costs for the cabin were amazingly low, they really escalated in the *food* category. Thoreau reported living on twenty-seven cents a week! He was largely a vegetarian and grew most of his food, such as his famous beans, Indian corn, rye, a few peas, pumpkins, potatoes, and beets. He occasionally ate a mess of fish or a woodchuck. He also made a "satisfactory dinner" from a dish of purslane. His overall bill for an eight-month period was $8.74!

To all this culinary economy, I have only one reply: "Good for Thoreau, but it won't work for me."

In the first place, I'm not a vegetarian, and don't wish to be. Secondly, the soil has become too acidified, and my woods are too dense to farm successfully. Local fish have largely disappeared because of acid rain. Woodchucks are scarce in the wilderness. To hunt small or large game or waterfowl for food means buying licenses, adhering to set seasons, and obeying bag limits. Wild animals and birds are no longer available year-round, as they were when Thoreau lived. Many edible weeds do not grow in the dense Adirondack forests.

I can't begin to estimate what my food costs were at Thoreau II for a week, much less eight months. With a full freeze-dried dinner (main course, vegetable, and dessert) running about $8.00 for two; a jar of peanut butter around $1.95, and can of espresso, $3.50, I'm sure I ate for $8.74 a *day*. Of course, I could do so for less, using canned goods, grains, rice, and water. Probably the only three items Thoreau and I would have had in common in our menus are salt, water, and molasses (though I substituted maple syrup). Even here I found a major discrepancy in prices. Thoreau spent three cents for an unspecified amount of salt (probably a pound), but it cost me twenty-five cents. His jug of molasses (no doubt a gallon) totaled $1.73, while maple syrup runs close to $25.00 a gallon.

All in all, it wasn't easy, or even advisable, to copy his cabin at Walden or to live like Thoreau completely. I didn't want to skimp on some of today's hi-tech gadgets that are so superior. For instance, I wouldn't give up my chain saw, aluminum canoe, canned dog food, manual typewriter, or fiberglass insulation in order to duplicate old-fashioned facsimiles or methods. I can give myself more time to write and explore, and I have more comfort than Thoreau did.

In summary, I found it was possible to build and furnish a tiny dwelling in the woods for about four times what it cost Thoreau 140 years ago.* (It meant cutting my own trees to do so, and this does *not* count buying and

---

*Interestingly, copies of the most famous small house in American literature are getting costly. Roland Robbins, the man who discovered Thoreau's cabin, recently paid three thousand dollars for his reproduction. The Thoreau Society in Concord, Massachusetts, built a replica for four thousand dollars, and the state of Massachusetts paid seven thousand dollars for it in the summer of 1956.

repairing a chain saw, transporting some materials by truck to my jumpoff point, or owning two canoes and paddles.) I discovered that good neighbors, willing friends, native ingenuity, and shrewd Yankee scrounging ability are still alive and well in the Northeast. What's come between a person's individual freedoms in the years between 1845 and 1985 is local and state bureaucracies, taxes and laws. What's come both to help and to hinder a person's wilderness life is high technology and all its gadgets.

Nevertheless, when I placed the key to Thoreau II on a length of rawhide and hung it around my neck, I felt a bond between my wee cabin and me as strong as between parents and their new offspring.

HENRY THOREAU'S EXPENSES

Board (mostly shanty boards purchased from neighbor)	$ 8.03	1/2
Refuse shingles for roof, sides (from neighbor)	4.00	
Laths	1.25	
2 secondhand windows with glass	2.43	
Door (probably made from boards)	—	
1,000 old bricks	4.00	
2 casks lime	2.40	
Hair (?)	.31	
Mantle-tree iron	.15	
Nails	3.90	
Chalk	.01	
Hinges and screws	.14	
Latch	.10	
1 japanned lamp	?	
1 washbowl and dipper	?	
Transportation ("I carried a good part on my back")	1.40	
	$28.12	1/2
Oil and some household utensils	2.00	
	$30.12	1/2
State tax	—	
Local building permit	—	
Adirondack Park Agency Permit	—	
TOTAL	$30.12	1/2

ANNE LABASTILLE'S EXPENSES

17 one-by-eight-inch boards	
(scrounged from construction site)	$ .00
12 particle board sheets	
(scrounged from construction site)	.00
Plastic sheeting	3.99
4 secondhand glass windows (given by neighbors)	.00
2 secondhand doors (given by neighbors)	.00
4 firebricks for stove (from Rod)	.00
1 potbellied stove (from Mary)	.00
Stovepipes, damper, cap	26.82
Asbestos wallboard	
(left over from West of the Wind)	.00
Nails and spikes	9.76
4 each two-by-fours and two-by-ones lumber	12.04
Hinges, hasp, padlock, hook	10.21
1 roll fiberglass insulation (for chinking)	12.77
1 chainsaw file	1.79
Steel roofing sheets (from dump)	.00
1 kerosene lamp	3.99
1 tin pail	2.89
1 sink (from trash pile in Miami)	.00
10 feet sink pipe, drain with plastic connector, ring	8.12
Roof paint	4.88
Transportation (I carried everything on my back)	.00
Oil, kerosene, chainsaw gas	10.00
	$110.98
State tax	7.77
Local building permit	10.00
Adirondack Park Agency permit (postage only)	2.00
TOTAL	$130.75

SAUNTERING AROUND LILYPAD LAKE

I began living at Thoreau II during the harvest moon of September. Maroon maples cloaked the hills. Nights were chilly, but frost had not yet touched the land. At dawn Lilypad Lake was muffled with mists. As the sun rose behind Lilypad Mountain, the mist lifted in streamers until the water shone like a mirror. Day after day was warm and sunny. The swallows, swifts, hummingbirds, and warblers had headed south. Canada geese were still to come. It seemed a magical interlude between summer and autumn, and it was almost two years to the day since I'd started my wilderness cabin.

This fall was my season of fruition. I wanted to spend several days at Thoreau II writing, walking, and contemplating nature and enjoying a respite from all the intrusions, delays, injuries, demands, and frustrations of the past years. When I spoke to Mike about this, he was less than enthusiastic.

"What if you get hurt way back in there?" was his immediate reaction. "No one would know. I can't be with you. Several big cases are pending over the next two weeks."

I knew my safety was foremost in the mind of this physician (and rightly so), but somehow I'd expected and needed his encouragement. As before, when I'd moved into West of the Wind, I felt certain apprehensions about being alone so far from other humans.

"Why can't you write at your big cabin?" Mike went on. "Or better yet, come on down here early this year. You know I love to have you spend the winters with me. Why not the fall?"

He had missed the point entirely. "Two reasons," I tried to explain. "I want to savor Thoreau Two after all the time and headaches it's taken to build it. Secondly, I *need* to go there to write, *really write*, my book undisturbed. It's the same way you *have* to be in a hospital to work, not a shopping mall. Well, I *have* to be in the woods, not in town. Don't you see?"

He didn't; he couldn't; he wouldn't. There were too many differences between our respective professions. The conflict hung there unresolved. Yet I was determined to go. The words of Isaiah (54:2–3) came to mind and supported my decision: "Enlarge the place of thy tent, and let them stretch forth the curtains of thine habitations: spare not, lengthen thy cords, and strengthen thy stakes; for thou shalt break forth on the right hand and on the left. . . ."

Therefore, on a golden afternoon I made my preparations. Packing some perishable food, my pistol, books and notes, cameras and film, binoculars, and the dog whistle in a pack basket, I hiked up and settled in. Just before nightfall, I went down to the lake for a bucket of water and a look around. I felt somewhat forlorn. Yet I was in a far better state of mind than when I'd moved into West of the Wind. The years of working and living in the woods had strengthened my self-confidence and courage in ways that could never have happened in a city and with a city job. And my emotional attachment to a fine man had filled the lonesome corners of my heart.

Coming back up the knoll, I looked at the tiny cabin and gasped in surprise. The candles flickering on my desk cast a soft glow throughout the room. At the same time peach and cream reflections from the sunset shone on the narrow-paned windows. My retreat looked like a little shrine. I stood transfixed. Deep inside I knew I'd been right to come here.

Stepping carefully over the log sill so as not to spill water on the floor, I set the bucket inside the Miami sink. Then I filled a pan with water for the dogs and took several long swallows from my dipper. Finally I stood in the center of that room, letting the silence envelop me and the smell of new wood fill my nostrils. I could scarcely believe that the retreat was finished. I was so used to hauling, pounding, measuring, sawing that I hardly knew what to do with myself.

Then practical matters motivated me. The dogs were hungry. My stomach was rumbling, too. The cabin was cooling down. Sleeping bags had to be unrolled and fluffed up. All the normal cabin chores were waiting here. After everyone had been fed and the stove fire was crackling, I sank down in the rocker and threw the old patchwork quilt over my legs.

The next morning a young white-throated sparrow greeted me with an amusing rendition of the normal "Sam Peabody-Peabody-Peabody" song. Like an adolescent choirboy whose voice is changing, this sparrow cracked on high notes, skipped some low ones, and chimed a whimsical new white-throated melody. An incandescence grew in the southeast as the sun rose. The pearly fog trembled, turned pinkish. A long ruddy duck traced a smooth arrow on the platinum surface. 'Kika whined, and Condor thumped his foot on the floor in a morning scratch. Time to get up! I bounced down the ladder and was smothered with doggie licks, kisses, sideswipes, and tail wags. Time for a swim!

I knew that wading off the point would mean sinking into the slimy lake bottom. Yet like Thoreau, bathing in a pond every morning was practically "a religious exercise, and one of the best things which I did." I decided to enter from a rock by the beaver dam and outlet. I slipped in without a splash and swam toward the main lake with only my head out of water. Suddenly a brown head appeared around the little point, coming my way. The two dogs were quiet, watching from shore. I continued toward the animal, and it toward me. It was a small beaver. No doubt it had finished its night's feeding and was headed to its newly mudded lodge on Birch Pond.

At twenty feet away I could see its nose, whiskers, eyelashes, and perky short ears. Its eyes glinted brightly in the strengthening light. Beavers have fairly poor sight, and this one was no exception. It finally slowed down about fifteen feet away, sniffed, and turned sideways as if to watch better this beaverlike object sculling near its dam. I trod water. It stopped, slapped its tail hard, and dived. What a way to start the day.

Over Cuban espresso, bread and jam, I resolved to saunter around Lily-pad Lake my first day at the cabin. Thoreau speaks of "sauntering" as the art of taking walks. (The word is derived from the Middle Ages, when idle people went to *Sainte Terre*, or the Holy Land.) A saunterer was a seeker of holy lands. Such walkers, says Thoreau, belong to a fourth estate, outside of those of church, state, and people. That's how I felt as I viewed the "fourth estate" stretched out before me—now clear and mirroring the burgundy-colored hills. I was free, unobtainable, detached from the other three estates, and open to adventure.

Heading east, I crossed the outlet of Lilypad Lake and descended through a tawny tangle of ostrich ferns. Rust, tan, and gold fronds nodded in the slight breeze. Individual leaflets were curled up from frost almost like the fertile fetal fiddleheads of spring seeking the sun. Crimson maple leaves had fallen on some horizontal fronds and lay like rubies on topaz.

I picked up a dim trail along the eastern lakeshore and moved easily through sunny hardwoods. Red squirrels chattered as we passed, and a pileated woodpecker tapped noisily on a yellow birch stub. Along the way, three marks made by humans caught my eye. One, a crumbling wooden sign pointed the way to a distant pond. It had been nailed up decades earlier. Then there was a shiny yellow and blue Department of Environmental Conservation metal poster, indicating I had crossed into a wilderness area. And lastly, a rusty tin can with a wire handle beside a nameless brook. Someone had drunk here years ago and left this simple dipper. I put it in my pack to hang on the cabin wall. It was a memento of the third estate, which it seemed I could not avoid.

Where the brook and trail turned to climb a hill, I left and sought the shore again. Plowing into the marsh that skirts Lilypad, I headed for a tiny "island" barely connected to land by watery tussocks of sedges. On its south side I stripped off my shirt and lay down on a warm, sunny rock. The dogs curled up on cool spagnum moss.

We were not alone. Dozens upon dozens of dragonflies performed aerial maneuvers above the marsh. Their transparent wings glittered in the sunshine as whole squadrons zoomed straight ahead over the water as if in pursuit of something. Pairs circled, dodged, hovered, and locked together in embraces which still permitted them to fly straight or in circles. Lone dragonflies darted like miniature projectiles in all directions. The lake was alive with these insects.

As I sat watching and munching a Bartlett pear, one black-and-blue-striped fellow, long as a Tiparillo, lit on my hand. At first I thought he coveted my fruit, but then I saw his bottle green head and proboscis were busy mincing up a beetle he'd just captured. He devoured the entire insect as I watched, inches away, face-to-face. Snack over, he zipped off after new prey. Then it came to me. The dragonflies are the A-10s of the insect world: predatory, businesslike, noisy, but tactically brilliant. In fact, their motto could be the same as that of the Air National Guard jet fighter pilots who have disturbed the peace at Black Bear Lake: "Get Ugly Early."

Maybe there's little basic difference between insects and humans. One attacks prey directly to eat and survive; the other captures natural resources and the financial wealth of its victims.

As I was mulling over this observation, three new signs of humankind intruded. One was the noon whistle from the Hawk Hill fire hall, six crow-miles away, blown in by the south wind. Another was a silvery military jet spiraling fifty thousand feet in the air. And third was the distant drone of a helicopter. No doubt it was taking water samples from the state's acid raid survey.

Still another reminder of civilization met my eyes as I was dozing through the noon hour. Many dramatic-looking stumps and snags, long dead, rose around the tiny island. Some had been cut about four feet above the ground (or snow level), just like the ones at Birch Pond. Evidently the same lumberjack of winters past had come here to harvest his cabin posts of tamarack and rafters of spruce. I was not the first to cut trees on this land.

As I finished sunning, I saw that the rock beneath me was covered with curly brown lichens. I peeled some off, popped them in my mouth, and let them soak up saliva. When they were as chewy as cheese curds, I swallowed them. They were a cross among mushrooms, brewer's yeast, and consommé in taste. They *might* fill a hungry person up—if he or she were short of peanut butter sandwiches.

Lunch and lichens over, I continued to skirt the lake to its inlet. A brooklet entered from a swampy area above. Deciding to take a look at that, I entered a hemlock and balsam thicket. A blue jay rose, screaming alarm, and a minute later a ruffed grouse thundered away. Condor and Chekika scrambled after them.

Ahead of me I saw a new beaver pond with a perfect reflection of autumn trees. The animals had been busy, for a dam about five hundred feet long ponded up two acres of water. Scarlet and yellow leaves fell sporadically onto the placid surface. Their ends curled up like the tops of my two canoes. As the breeze blew erratically, they all first veered one way, then sailed slowly back toward me like a little brigade of voyageurs.

Back at the head of the lake I found a small sandy area and decided to swim. I took off the dogs' collars and my clothes, and we waded in. The bottom was not as slimy as on the other side, but still, clouds of muck billowed up under us. The sun was hot and the water refreshing as we dogpaddled around. Then the distant sound of a seaplane came to my ears.

I began to swim for shore, but the muck slowed me down. I'd barely reached the sand when a plane flew over the hill, veered, and headed straight toward me. There wasn't time to throw on a stitch, so I called the dogs, crouched down, and pulled them in close to me. The pilot flew directly overhead and waggled his wings. I hung my head and hoped he'd overlook the assortment of black, tan, and blond coloration below—but I doubt it. So much for sauntering in the nude!

Now I headed back along the steep north-facing slope under the brooding brow of Lilypad Mountain. The difference in micro-climate was instantly noticeable. I felt as though I were climbing into a giant terrarium. The air was cool and damp on this shady slope. Each stone was blanketed with lush moss; every fallen log was a garden of partridgeberry, spaghnum, and baby hemlocks. The forest was as wild and untouched as any in the Adirondacks. Birches, three and four feet in diameter, soared against the blue September sky. Some of their roots spraddled rocks and formed crannies where a racoon could easily hide. Huge hemlocks and spruces stood ramrod straight above a profusion of ferns.

I was elated to find this patch of primeval forest and grateful that it could never be cut. While I agree that some trees should be harvested like crops—be it corn or cotton or conifers—I don't think all of them should be considered crops. I've walked through too many clear-cuts, shelterwoods, and selective logging jobs. I've seen the berry bushes and pioneer trees slowly fill in the gaps. Although regeneration over decades will heal the scars, most lumbered sites look and are ravaged. The trade-offs—whether in pulp, paper, veneer, furniture, or firewood—can never quite atone for lumbering a virgin tract of trees. Sheer aesthetics, high-quality water, and ecological balance are often more precious to maintain.

It also grieves me every time I see discarded newspapers blowing down city streets or stacks of paper plates and cups in the garbage. These items were once trees. To have the forest I was sauntering through come to such an end would have been infinitely saddening.

The sound of water gurgling down the slope reached my ears. On investigation, I found a whole series of crystal-clear rivulets, half aboveground, half under, flowing downhill. Under the root system of a falling giant I found what I'd been hoping for: a spring hole. Now I could come by canoe to fill jugs with icy, clean water rather than use the lake or outlet. I stopped to move some stones and deepen the spring hole.

Chickadees and juncos flitted and chattered in the balsams. As I worked and the dogs rested, a young mink scampered along the shoreline. When it caught our scent, it hissed angrily. Poised and unfrightened, he did an agitated little tap dance atop a rock at the sight of us. The youngster was still a fuzzy charcoal color rather than the sleek mahogany of an adult. As the mink saw Condor rise, it thought better of it and slithered into a labyrinth of tiny tunnels.

The slope steepened, and a rock face began. Gradually, it heightened and flattened until I reached a place where a cliff rose twenty-five feet. The side was slick with moisture and moss, glistening like green Vaseline. Tiny trickles of water dripped tirelessly onto an emerald blanket of sphagnum at its base. The sun was all but blocked out. I shivered. This could be a spooky place on a rainy, windy night. But the brilliant blaze of an orange maple overhanging the cliff and a few lances of sunlight dispelled my quivers. I felt that I'd penetrated deep into the private root zone of Adirondack rock.

Stumbling through the narrow gully, I came face-to-face with an ancient blaze and trace of a trail. Could this be part of the old route those early hikers had followed to feast on homemade pies and tea at Black Bear Lake? It headed in the general direction of Thoreau II, so we took it. Witch hobble had grown up luxuriantly along the way. I pushed past leaves as large as pie plates, colored in enchanting shades of pink, lime green, vermilion, chartreuse, oxblood, olive, and magenta.

To my surprise, I came upon the same outlaw camp that had supplied my plates and cups for the cabin—how long ago? Bits of black plastic were still plastered to the ground. I ripped them up and found four frying pans. I'd overlooked them before, and surely this was proof that no one had been here for eight years. One pan was Teflon and in good shape. Another was stainless steel which folded in half for boiling or lay flat for frying.

The pans immediately came into use. Condor and 'Kika were ravenous after the long bushwhack, so I prepared their supper in the big Teflon one. Carrots and beets went in the other to boil for my supper.

As we all ate, the sky was slowly glazing over with silver and the fitful south wind was dying. Afterward I slid the canoe into the water, loaded the dogs, and began to circle the lake in the direction opposite to my earlier saunter. As I paddled, water bugs that had been invisible on the lake surface sprang alive and zig-zagged away from me. Each one sparkled like a sequin. At least *they* throve on the acidic conditions. Wave after wave swarmed ever father away. No wonder certain ducks and mergansers could survive here, at least temporarily, on this abundant food supply. A few fragile midges hung in the still air. Others lay dead on the water. More duck food.

I reached the standing dead trees and paddled among them as through a watery petrified forest. The low September sun hung above the far shore. In its slanted rays, every furrow, crack, jagged edge, and knot stood out on the snags like sculptured pewter. Under the standing trees their fallen limbs lay intact, pickled (it seemed) in the clear acidified water. The sun set. A lemon backwash was left in the sky. One star stood out overhead. A stray robin sang its woodnote sleepily from shore. Wood toads began their evening chirping. A lone bat skimmed the surface for fallen bugs. Each time it snared one there was a tiny noise like a cigarette falling into the water—zifffft.

The lake was cloaked in austere purple and seemed larger than by day. In the last light a pair of hooded mergansers whirred down from the silvery sky and parted the water neatly in a long V for their night's rest. As I turned toward Thoreau II, both dogs were asleep in the bottom of the canoe, snoring gently. When I pulled up on shore, they woke and leaped out. The only sound now was the outlet faintly purling over the beaver dam.

Then from far off came the honking of geese. The first of the season! They were high and traveling fast. As always, tears spilled from my eyes at the thought of facing winter and all the dangers which lay ahead for those gallant birds until they rested for the season. I felt my arms beating like their wings, air rushing through the pinions. I saw the lakes, burgundy and black below their tired breasts. I willed them to turn toward my retreat and settle on Lilypad for the night. I yearned to hear them "lumbering in the dark with a clangor and awhistling of wings," as Thoreau had when they came into Walden Pond. But they moved on. Others would come and find refuge here. I turned to the cabin and went in.

Later in my loft I thought back on the day. If this was sauntering—by foot or by paddle—then truly I'd spent a day in *Sainte Terre*—my holy land. As I fell asleep, the constellation Cassiopeia crept through a cleft among the conifers and gazed calmly down upon the cabin.

Martha Reben

Martha Reben

Martha Rebentisch went to the Adirondacks seeking a cure for tuberculosis and found herself. In 1927 the Saranac Lake cure was the most popular for people like Martha. At sixteen, she had discovered that she was afflicted with an advanced case of TB. Her mother had died of the disease when Martha was six, and her father, a superintendent for a jewelry concern, was struggling to raise his three daughters in Manhattan where Martha had been born. When her condition was first discovered, she went to a farm to recover; after two months she returned to the city and suffered a relapse. Within a few months she was in a sanatorium, but after a year and a half she returned to the city only to have another, more serious relapse. Finally she was sent to Saranac Lake. In February 1931, after enduring three years of being bed-ridden and two nerve operations, including one which collapsed one of her diseased lungs, she was faced with the prospect of more surgery which it was hoped would save her life. Out of desperation, despair, pain and boredom, and with a self-determination which was to become characteristic of her, Martha decided that she had to get out of the hospital environment if she was going to recover.

Providentially, Fred Rice of Saranac Lake, a robust woodsman and guide-boat builder by trade, had at that time also reached a revolutionary conclusion regarding the modern treatment of TB. Rice had for years been interested in the sorts of cures and regimen used at the sanatorium and how far they deviated from the treatment that Dr. Edward Trudeau himself had devised. The fifty-five year old mountaineer was an advocate of the outdoors as a cure. He placed an advertisement in the local paper seeking a patient who had not been getting well with routine care and making himself available to take such an invalid into the forest to live and—he hoped—to recover.

Martha responded to his ad, and although he had not thought of taking a woman into the woods, her case fit his requirements, and she was persuasive. In June they went to Weller Pond to camp, Martha riding twelve miles to the site on a cot and mattress across the seats of Rice's boat because she was too weak to sit up. By the end of the first week, she was able to walk around camp unaided. Hers was a remarkable recovery. Ten years later, when she finally consulted her doctors again, she was free of TB.

At Weller Pond, where she slept in the open under a great pine at lakeside, she often camped alone when Rice was away. She learned to hunt and fish as well as to find her way through the trackless forest with a compass. She kept a shotgun nearby when in camp alone, but never needed it; eventually Rice confided that it hadn't ever been loaded. Although he taught her how to hunt deer, she went one whole season without shooting any of the seven she saw. By nature gentle anyway, she had come to see the pleasure in living in harmony with the creatures of the mountain forest. Eventually she convinced Fred to give up hunting too.

She enrolled in courses in English and journalism at the Saranac Study and Craft Guild, an organization formed to give training to recovering tuberculosis patients. She began keeping a journal, collecting material and musing on paper which, after twenty-eight years, became her first book, *The Healing Woods*. When she was too weak to sit up at the typewriter, Rice learned to type her manuscripts. In 1941, Martha's heart, which had been sorely strained as a result of the TB treatments, forced them to move their camp to a level place on Hungry Bay (now Rice Point). With Martha's aid, Rice put together his own story and speculations about the efficacy of nature as healer in "Fifty Years In a Health Resort" which appeared in 1937. Martha herself finished the first book in the autobiographical series about her life in the woods and Saranac Lake; in 1952, *The Healing Woods* was published. There followed *The Way of the Wilderness* in 1955 and finally *A Sharing of Joy* in 1963. Her publishers abbreviated her name to Reben. The books sold well, and were even published abroad, but brought her no fortune. In 1956 Cornelius Vanderbilt Whitney took an interest in Reben's work because he wanted to use her life story as the basis for a movie to be made by his motion picture company. He paid her for an option on her books, but because of his own marital difficulties, the movie was never made. Reben used the money to move herself and Rice, then in his 80s, closer to town. When she died in 1964 she left an estate which went into trust to care for her dear friend and guide, Fred Rice. It is mute testimony to his theories about healing that she died not of TB but from the displacement of her heart and esophagus caused by early treatment of her disease.

Her books remain as testament not only to her cure but to the emerging spirit of independence and self-reliance which turning to the woods gave Reben. The city-born woman truly reclaimed her self when she went into the mountain wilderness to live. On her first day alone at the campsite she noted her isolation, so different form the sanatorium's: "For the rest of the day, no matter what contingency arose, I had no one to depend upon but myself. It was the first time in my life."[1]

Like Thoreau, she simplified. Away from the enclosure and constraint of the hospital, the "cloistered life" as she called it, she stripped to essentials, often sun-bathing nude and always eating as simply as possible.[2] This was a distinct change from the medical regimen of forced eating to gain weight: "At noon I ate bread and cheese and drank lake water, for I had already discovered that in the woods one spent as little time on meals as possible, and that far from stores with well-stocked food counters, one ate primarily to appease hunger rather then for delectation."[3] After only a week her new intimacy with the woodland brought her to immersion, a metaphoric baptism in the purifying life of the mountains:

> I had already noticed how perfectly the yellow and brown plaid shirt which I was wearing matched the dappled spots of sunshine on the ground. I must have been almost invisible, for the wild partridges to have ignored me so completely. My hair was nearly the color of the reddish-brown bark of the Norway pine against which I leaned, and my skin, now tanned by a week's sun, was almost as brown. Only the blue of my eyes betrayed me. I was careful not to move.[4]

This identification with the natural world was not only liberation from disease and the confinement it had imposed on her. The red-haired beauty had finally found a self she could rely on and be proud of:

> The wilderness did more than heal my lungs, however. While it dwarfed me by its immensity and made me conscious of my insignificance yet it made me aware of the importance of being an individual, capable of thinking and feeling not what was expected of me, but only what my own reasoning told me was true. It taught me fortitude and self-reliance, and

> with its tranquility it bestowed upon me something which would sustain
> me as long as I lived: a sense of the freshness and the wonder which life in
> natural surroundings daily brings and a joy in the freedom and beauty and
> peace that exist in a world apart from human beings.[6]

Her father's visit to her at Rice's home was another turning point
for her. He wanted her home now that she was somewhat better and
one of her sisters had left home to make a career for herself. Implicit
in the scene is the contrast between Fred Rice, who Martha called
Gramps, and Ernest Rebentisch. The latter was coarse and self-
involved; Rice was kindly and generous. Reben chose to stay. Her
decision was weighted by the disparity she saw between the values she
and Rice held and those of her father, although she did not blame
Rebentisch for his lack of sympathy.

> In his busy life there was little time for soul-searching, and how could he be
> expected to understand the change that had taken place in me on the
> pond?[6]

Martha had been adopted; from accounts of those who knew them,
Fred and Martha became increasingly like father and daughter.

Soon after she committed herself to staying in Saranac Lake, she
moved into a cottage of her own for the winter. She reconstructed the
tiny domicile in a manner reminiscent of Thoreau's, though not
building it from the ground up but creating a home where there had
before been only boards and lathe. It represented the creation of her
own self and was her first place to call her own. She relished the new-
ness about it.

> Nobody, I felt sure, had been born here, and nobody had died here. . . .as
> though the little house had been waiting all these years for its history to be
> made, as though its past still lay somewhere in the future.[7]

Her emergence as a new, independent being continued at an aston-
ishing pace. She decided to finish the high school education that
had been cut short by her disease, but could not attend school
because of health form requirements, so she began a course of self-
education. When her allowance money was drastically reduced by her
father, she sought ways to make a living in Saranac Lake as waitress
and hairdresser until she realized, "I walked along Main Street glancing into stores and offices, and it seemed to me, as it had to Thoreau,

that I saw the occupants doing penance in a thousand remarkable ways."[8] When she finds the work she can do unsuitable, she decides, "I along with my fellow townsmen, had somehow sold my birthright for a mess of pottage,"[9] and she determines to be free of that kind of enclosure as surely as she had the hospital. When she is asked to curl the hair of a corpse, she flees, resolving to go back to the woods and write. When she arrives at Weller Pond she finds

> this was the peace beyond expression I had come so far to find, for which I was renouncing human companionship, many comforts and every luxury, but I did not think the price was too high.[10]

The choice to separate from her father and live independently signalled another break with the traditional values of her early life. Her family seems to have been Jewish, but by the time Reben was hospitalized she felt herself freed from any such definition of spiritual identity. According to Rice's sister, who knew Martha, whenever she was asked her religion she replied "humanitarianism" because it always confused the questioner. In the second book there is a streak of powerful spirituality that grows stronger with each chapter. It is, however, not at the surface of her text any more than Thoreau's was. It shimmers just beneath the clear prose which describes and narrates the daily wonders of her life in the woods. She is a realistic writer, a recorder of the minutiae she observes, catching the rhythm of days and domestic detail of first sustaining and then building a life in the open air.

The lure of the wilderness for Reben was somewhat different from that which drew other women, but not entirely. She ruminated on the value of wilderness, looking at a huge log at her feet:

> To the wilderness around us thirty years meant only a tiny bit of decay and replacement, a few more inches on the girth to the trees, a little more duff on the forest floor. Out here, time, as we measured it, seemed to stand still, and perhaps that, more than anything else, was what men found so sustaining and so seductive.[11]

Her notion is not so far from Thoreau's own: "Time is but the stream I go a-fishing in." There is also the impulse to be primary, essential, solitary in a place where no other human has been, for the purity of it. Looking for a nameless pond to explore, Reben thought "I might be the first woman to stand on its shore. The idea appealed to me, probably because there are so few places left in the world about which one can claim this distinction."[12] The search for a virgin, self-created space reflects the writer's sense of her own newly-created self.

The excerpts which follow, taken from her second and third books, show Reben speculating on the meaning of her life in the mountains, her place in the scheme of things, and the relationship of human life to the planet's. The first selection is taken from *The Way of the Wilderness*. Compared with LaBastille's account of her night on a mountaintop, it reveals a common experience of woman's place in the world—separate, small, but in touch with transcendental oneness. What is so remarkable about Reben's account is the fact of her going to the summit at all, the attempt as well as the achievement. In "To A Waterfowl," the writer's interest in the domestic features of wilderness life appear. The ideas of marriage and mating run just below the surface in her work. When she hired a handyman to help her rebuild her cottage, she thought of having him carry her over the threshold, an image that reflects not only her physical exhaustion but her concern with being part of the natural mating rhythms she witnessed around her. Yet when she met a young man (the "Eric" of her book) at the Study Guild and decided to marry him, she felt terrible ambivalence about giving up her solitude and thereby some of herself. Reben fictionalized his death in *The Way of the Wilderness* by creating an auto accident which almost conveniently kept her from having to choose between matrimony and the wilderness. The young man was actually an outpatient with TB who, after five years with Martha, died of a sudden relapse in his disease. In her prose Reben is intensely conscious of the mating and nurturing habits of the wildlife, sometimes looking for domesticity where there was none and ascribing motives which were human rather than animal. Her maternal relation to the mountain creatures was manifest in her nurturing various birds and animals that inhabited her campsites and cottage. At first she tried sentimentally to meddle with their habits, but soon she learned that she was interfering with natural processes. She quickly came to recognize the need for humans to stand out of the way and simply protect that environment which enhanced these processes. She eventually bought a thirty–five acre tract of wetlands for a waterfowl sanctuary. When her father sent her two hundred dollars for necessary dental work, she spent it on the sanctuary instead. The birds needed a place for themselves as much as she did. In "The Bears of Fat Fish Pond" Reben is at work again describing the curious animal life around her and the ways in which human beings impinge on it. Each piece demonstrates Reben's style—clear and direct, with precise renderings of color and texture and little use of poetic devices. The spareness of her style underlines the sure simplicity of her life renewed and reclaimed at Weller Pond.

Then after loading the little pack basket with a quilt, a flashlight, some woolen underclothes, a sandwich and a tin cup, I set out to find that all the sharpness had gone out of the air, leaving it as mild as in later summer. The wind was still blowing steadily out of the southwest, the direction from which our finest weather usually came. And although one little puff of cloud had come up over Stony Creek Mountain the rest of the sky was clear and blue.

I climbed the first rise and crossed the brook, quieter now than it had been a few days earlier. The basket on my back proved unexpectedly heavy, and after a few minutes I sat down to rest.

When I went on, I passed through a balsam swamp, full of tangled windfalls, and then on the other side of the trail climbed sharply. Before I parted from the brook, I took a drink of water, thinking it would be my last chance, but the trail wound so that I came upon it again unexpectedly a few hundred feet higher up. Being thirsty, I drank some more.

The nearer I got to the top, the steeper the climbing became; and, although my one lung worked valiantly, I had to stop often to clear the spots dancing before my eyes. I had never climbed a mountain before, so when I saw the open sky ahead and above me, I thought the next rise would be the last. But after I reached it I found that beyond that was another, and when I stood, breathless, on top of that I found still another awaiting me.

In spite of my pounding heart and throbbing temples and the spots before my eyes, I became more and more elated as the trees fell away from me and the top of the mountain came in sight. The final fifty feet was steep and rocky, but at last I stepped out of a clump of stunted poplars and birches onto the bare, rocky top, and, though I was gasping, I felt that I should never breathe more freely than I did at this moment.

I was wholly unprepared for a scene so far-reaching and spectacular. To the west stretched the long upper lake with its bays and islands, the water glistening in the evening sunlight. To the north was another strip of blue which I thought might be Lake Clear. The green slopes fell away at my feet and rose again, hill beyond hill, dark green in the foreground, the green fading to blue, then lightening shade on shade until it almost merged with the sky.

When I had caught my breath I made my way through a little strip of small poplars shutting off my view to the south and came out on a rocky prominence overlooking the pond and Round Lake, where another panorama stretched before me. Here the wind blew strongly but below me the pond was dark green, almost black. I let the wind blow against my face for a while and then I returned to where I had left my basket and began gathering wood for a fire. There were dry twigs everywhere. I laid my fire against a big boulder but I did not light it. There was a boat down in Saginaw Bay in the upper lake looking no bigger than a toy.

I sat down and ate my sandwich. The sun sank out of sight, and for a while the whole immense landscape glowed rosy purple. Across the sky a banner was flung, thin and wispy, faintly pink, all that was left of the puff of cloud that had come up over Stony Creek two hours before.

Slowly the color deepened to purple, the sky darkened and the stars came out. A peace, profound beyond expression, lay over the woods and waters and a little of it found its way into my troubled being.

I drew the old quilt around me, feeling dwarfed by so much space and beauty. The stars brightened and to the north I could see a few lights, one of them seeming to hang on the tip of a mountain. The only sound was the wind rustling through the branches of the shrubby trees behind me, as I sat and watched the wilderness merge into the blue of night.

When the earth disappeared in darkness, the heavens took over. For the first time in my life I had an inkling of what infinity meant. As I gazed at the brilliant display of star beyond star I became lost in the immensity of space, almost worshipfully aware of the force which had formed me, the woods and lakes and mountains as well as the galaxies and nebulae shining before my awestruck eyes.

After a while there was a lessening of the darkness below me, a glint of silver on the water. The moon was coming up. Everything was so still, so un-moving, that when a meteor streaked across the sky and exploded it was as shocking as a stab of physical pain.

Then the moon was in sight, looking awesomely near at eye level, not flat and bright as it usually did, but like the tremendous, shining sphere it really was. The wilderness around me stood forth in its reflected radiance, vast, still, mysterious.

Something that sounded like a deer ran across the rock to my left and into the grove of trees behind me. I found the flashlight and the thin beam of light, absurdly feeble in the moonlight, revealed nothing and only emphasized the littleness of man's efforts against the forces of nature.

The isolation of the mountain top, surrounded by miles of moonlit woods and waters was indescribable. Solitude, for me had always been a silent communing with the forces around me from which I drew strength and serenity. Some of my pleasantest hours had been spent in this way, as one might spend them with a well-loved person.

But this solitude was so vast it was like putting into form the depth of isolation men feel within themselves, and it made poignant and real the knowledge that in life, as in death, man stands alone.

As I sat under the immense arch of the sky, looking down upon the slumbering wilderness, I knew that nothing, for me, would ever be the same again, that hereafter the bigness and littleness of things would forever have a changed significance.

I got up and lit my fire, and the blaze leaped up with a warmth that was more than physical. As it snapped and crackled, the fire pushed back the vastness and the loneliness and held me within the comfort of its dancing light. I wondered what the leaping flames must look like to anyone watching in the darkness below.

Nothing except the fire moved. I drew the quilt around me again, when I sat down. By what accident, I wondered, did I come to be sitting on this particular planet, part of a civilization to which I seemed forever doomed to remain an alien? Was existence as haphazard as it appeared? Was there any purpose to life? Someday, somewhere, would a pattern appear?

Something small, like a mouse, ran over my foot. The moon was high in the heavens now, but to the west I could see an area of sky without stars. Clouds were forming. If it turned cold I should have to leave the pond.

There was nothing left for me to do but to return to the little house outside the village, to the uneventfulness of countless snowy afternoons and evenings, and a quiet so unbroken that I could hear the icy pellets beating against the window panes and the wood shifting in the stove as it burned and fell apart. I would have to pick up the threads of my work where I had broken them off, but I would not exchange a single hour of my freedom for something I did not need. I would cut living to the bone and buy time for writing and studying with the things I did without.

❦

TO A WATERFOWL

To most persons a loon is only a sad, mournful, unearthly voice coming from some lonely, spruce-fringed mountain pond. To others he is a black dot far out in the center of the pond, a lover of solitude who disappears at sight of a boat.

He wasn't much more than that to me until the summer we camped on Fat Fish Pond. When we innocently began sharing the pond with a pair of these shy, difficult-to-approach water birds, we little dreamed to what an extent we should become involved in their daft and often desperate struggles with their surroundings before the summer was over.

A few mornings after we had become settled in camp we set out in the canoe for a jaunt around the mile-long pond, shimmering under a cloudless sky. It was one of those exquisite days in early spring when the sun puts a radiance on everything including even the rocks along the shores, and the air has a perfume that is sweeter than flowers.

We hadn't gone far when I had a confused vision of black and white as a loon slipped smoothly off her nest and disappeared under water. We'd have paddled right by without seeing her if she hadn't hit the water at the last moment that way.

Her nest, a remarkably shallow depression containing two khaki-colored eggs with dark brown spots, was on a pine log that must have been six feet in circumference, lying parallel to shore with the inner end submerged so that the log was entirely surrounded by water. It had lain there so long that it was overgrown with moss and low, scrubby bushes which served to conceal the nest on the farther end.

At first the loons, as though they had never seen people before, made a tremendous to-do whenever our canoe left the landing. But our diplomacy gradually won them over, and we came less and less under their verbal fire for having invaded what must have seemed to them their last stronghold. Even so, I think they looked upon us as something like unwelcome guests, whom they hoped wouldn't stay long.

Early one morning when the first light was just beginning to show, we heard their long-drawn, quavering cries which, as we listened, seemed to grow sharper and shriller with excitement. Evidently something more deadly than house guests was now troubling them.

We went out into the sharpened air and jumped in the canoe and paddled down the shore. A morning planet was still bright in the sky as I shone my light up and down the log. It picked out the glowing eyes and then the shaggy gray body of a coon. He was not on the log but on the boggy ground behind it, reaching around in the shallow water for crayfish or anything else edible he could find. He hadn't yet discovered the loon's nest, but I thought that, with their complete lack of strategy, it wouldn't be long before he did.

We drove him off, and later that morning had the satisfaction of seeing the loon back brooding her eggs. We gave her a wide berth, so as not to disturb her, although I longed to get close enough to see for myself whether she squatted on the nest, or whether as I had read, she rested alongside it and pulled the eggs close to her body with her wing, to brood them. The male, an affable, handsome bird, as big as a small goose, with checkered black-and-white plumage and a coal-black head, swam to intercept us and even followed us a little way.

Toward evening the wind began to blow. As it blew stronger and stronger I grew increasingly uneasy, remembering the coon, knowing that on such nights, under cover of noise and darkness, death walks abroad for all helplessly exposed ground-nesting birds.

Around daylight I awoke to hear the terrified squawking of a duck down the shore, and a few minutes later, as if in corroboration, the high, shrill cries of the loons.

There was still a swell on as we launched the canoe and quickly paddled down the shore to where their nest was. As soon as I shone my light, I saw that the coon had found the nest, and, unaware that these eggs were rarer than hens' teeth, was impudently eating them. (Records kept in Minnesota and British Columbia show that for 110 and 150 adults, respectively, only 21 young were hatched.) The loons were out in the middle of the pond calling imprecations down upon him, but we were too late to do anything to help them.

In the days that followed, we watched the loons anxiously. It was still early in the season. Would they nest again? Or had they sustained their heavy bodies on narrow-bladed wings, mile after weary mile, from some coastal lake where they had spent the winter, north to the place of their birth, only to be deprived of the joy of nesting?

For a while we feared the big birds had given up the unequal struggle against plunderers and had left the pond. Maybe they did shop around for a safer place to establish themselves, but no doubt they could not long forget the place that had imprinted itself on their earliest memories. Where water-fowl learn to fly is home to them. Anyway, they returned.

Along about the time the peep frogs left the marshes, we had reason to believe they were nesting again. We weren't able to find the nest, but when-ever we went out in the boat, now, one of them followed us, whooping in frantic protest if we came near what they evidently considered their side of the pond. They could easily outdistance our canoe, and if we came too close to them they dived (they are excellent divers, and have been caught in nets at depths of 200 feet on the Great Lakes), usually staying down an unbelievable length of time, then reappearing a couple of hundred feet away. Since both birds supposedly incubate the eggs and look much alike, we couldn't tell one from the other until we saw them together. The male was slightly larger.

Perhaps because he couldn't resist flattery, the male was a little less cautious and shy than his mate. More and more he took to swimming past camp, keeping a respectful distance from shore as he slyly watched to see how the neighbors were putting in their time.

Sometimes I went down to the water's edge, and in a burst of friendliness called to him in what was a very amateurish rendering of a loon's call. The first time I did it, he regarded me incredulously, and swam away so quickly and ungraciously that I wondered what I had said to offend him. But soon he began to show some interest, though a nontalking one. Then one day to my delight, he answered back. In no time, after that, we had what might be termed a speaking acquaintance, and we exchanged greetings many times a day. In fact he became so garrulous that he wouldn't let me finish, when I started to call, but would take the whoop right out of my mouth. And the shining of a light any time after dark was sure to get a response from him.

After awhile he overcame some of his distrust of strangers and swam in close enough to see what this baffling creature who sounded faintly like a loon looked like. As he gave me a careful inspection out of first one red eye then the other, pondering and sipping the while, I remembered having read that animals with good vision under water have poor sight out of it, and I wondered as what strange order of primate (lower than a loon, naturally) he would classify me. And what must he have thought of my puzzling ability to change color at will as I appeared in green one day and brown the next? He evidently found me completely baffling and therefore fascinating, because he came back again and again.

Loons are surprisingly vocal at all hours of the day, and especially on moonlit nights, when they sometimes race each other on the water, wailing and yodeling. (When the air is right, they can be heard two miles away.) In spite of the usually sad and mournful sounds our loons gave forth, no other bird I ever saw was as capable of enjoying itself, even when alone. I have watched this playboy, up to his eyes in lake water, sporting and frolicking as he wrestled with Neptune, showing unmistakably how much of a water bird he really was. It was more like watching a porpoise at play than a bird, as he dived exultantly through the waves, beat the water with his wings, rolled over first on one side then the other, exposing his gleaming white hull, then, back on an even keel, taking a running start, wings flapping, diving headlong into the pond again.

Sometimes he swam into a deep bay and played with the echoes, calling loudly, then listening for the echo to come back to him. Did he think it was another loon? I wondered.

It has been said that loons have carried underwater flight about as far as they can without actually losing aerial flight (as penguins have), and watching them, this seems easy to believe. Those who have seen them using their half-closed wings in swimming say they seem to be flying under water.

I soon noticed that our loon had a somewhat hooligan sense of humor. There were rafts of water bugs on the pond, and there was nothing he liked better than to submerge as silently and furtively as an enemy submarine and come up among a flock of carefree ducklings blissfully stuffing themselves on the bugs. He looked indescribably sinister as that big, coal-black head and long, sharp bill popped up out of the water. I did not blame the ducklings for screaming as, with outstretched wings and lowered head, he charged them; and I could almost *hear* him chortle as he watched their frantic efforts to beat him to shore.

Sometimes, in a strategy of concealment, he surfaced with only the curve of his back and the top of his head and, doubtless, his eyes above the water. He even managed his buoyancy control tanks so that he could swim that way when he wanted to prowl without being seen. If he had been trying to impersonate a big turtle at such times, he couldn't have looked more like one, and this, too, amused him, as he watched other waterfowl panic at sight of him. It is claimed that loons will sometimes kill ducklings, but I never saw him carry things that far.

Once, he made the mistake of popping up close to a flock of newly hatched ducklings still under the protective care of their mother. After a month of inactivity on her nest, the old duck, ripe for a fight, tangled with him, squawking like a Diesel locomotive at a crossing.

This was more than the loon had bargained for, and he nosed under, but he quickly appeared topside again, chagrined at having given way to a duck.

Strife had, by now, become essential to the mother duck's happiness, and, blind to danger, she rushed at him. This time he held his ground and they slugged it out with their wings until I hurried down to the water, clapping my hands and shouting to them to end their comic but unequal struggle.

I scolded the loon as the spunky little mother duck, a bit rattled by now, led her brood away, but he only turned and glanced back at me with what might have been a derisive look, hunching his shoulders and raising the down on his head and neck in a conscious gesture of self-importance.

(He loved the limelight, and he was becoming as audience-conscious as a movie star.) "Shucks, I never laid a webbed toe on her!" he seemed to say.

One still morning toward the middle of July when the shores were mirrored in the more magical and delicate and illusory blending of foliage and water, a slight distortion in the reflection over near the far shore brought the loons to my attention. What I saw sent me hurrying for the binocular.

When I focused the glass I found that the two dots on the water beside the older birds were baby loons. The new additions to the family looked so unbelievably tiny, that when I thought of the turtles, coons, minks, otters, hawks, and other enemies by which they were surrounded, I wouldn't have given a nickel for their chances of living long enough to become the size of their parents.

Almost from the day they were hatched, the babies would dive and stay under water a disturbingly long time. While I stood on shore and worried for fear they had been eaten by a big fish or turtle, their mother sat on the water as complacently as a young matron sitting on a park bench with her children romping about her.

Insofar as I knew, except when they were nesting, these waddlers, with their short legs set far back on their bodies to act as propellers, spent practically all their lives on water, and when they did fly, they hurled themselves through the air on their narrow wings (they have been clocked at sixty miles an hour) intent only on finding another body of water to light on. If, in bad judgment, they choose one that is too small for them to take off from (loons must run a long distance on the water before they can get into the air), they are trapped, and freeze or starve to death when cold weather sets in.

They even slept on the water, and I was curious, therefore, to know how the mother brooded her young (which left the nest soon after they were hatched), since all young birds need lots of warmth and rest.

One day, to my delight, I found out. I was watching the old loon through the binocular, and I saw that she was carrying both chicks on her back, one cuddled under each wing. Now and then a tiny head would rise above the upper side of her wing to look around. Patiently the mother sat on the water, barely moving her feet, glancing back over her shoulder from time to time to make sure the youngsters were taking their naps, apparently completely at peace with the disordered world around her. Loons are gentle and solicitous, if unsentimental parents, brooding, feeding, and defending their young with zest and devotion.

I saw one chick leave the protection of her wing, walk down her back and lean out over her tail and get himself a drink. His thirst quenched, he hurried back to bed, where it was warm.

Both parents shared in feeding their young, and in this, as in anything else they did, they seemed to take an almost frivolous enjoyment. All wild animals experience a joy in living that civilized man can only envy.

Whenever the old birds caught a fish, the young would paddle with anticipatory speed toward them, calling in tiny, bell-like voices, a sound so subtle and wild it required a keen ear to hear it. Often they came in so close I could see the glistening fish passed from one bill to another, a ritual that was accomplished so smoothly that one had to have a sharp eye to see it. Sometimes they crippled small fish with their strong, serrated bills, then released them so the young ones could have the fun of catching them, an effective way of teaching them to capture their own food.

I don't know how much untaught wisdom these young, web-footed creatures were born with, but the schooling started early and was both ancient and progressive. My impression was that the parents, besides teaching them to fish, drilled them frequently to respond to warning signals. Even our boat leaving the landing (harmless though they knew it to be) was sometimes used as an excuse to send the young loons into hiding, where they were expected to remain until the parents gave the "all clear" signal. These drills operated on the honor system (the parents followed our boat and called directions to the young, which were out of sight), and the young waterfowl learned to obey promptly. They had to, if they wanted to stay alive. It is the duckling that stops to look behind it that never grows up. The reason almost all wild things panic so easily is that they have to move first and consider afterward. With them flight takes the place of thought.

One afternoon I heard the loons crying havoc again. I went out and called to them, and their shrill replies confirmed that another of the welter of workaday disasters was befalling them.

When I hurried down to the water's edge I saw an eagle fly out of a big pine. It circled the pond, flying low over the loons, helplessly exposed out in the middle. They dived, every time it went over them, then popped right back up to call warnings to the babies, which were nowhere in sight.

I got in the canoe and quickly paddled out to them, because if the babies were trying to avoid the eagle by diving, too, I thought they would soon be exhausted. As soon as it saw me, the eagle hid among the branches of a pine farther down the pond.

Evidently the babies were well hidden. I watched the big bird in the pine, though, because I had once seen an eagle walking along the stones at the water's edge, apparently searching for some ducklings I knew were hidden close by. The loons were watching him, too, and they kept calling to the young ones to stay hidden.

After a while the king of birds, a rather shabby-looking king, I thought, flew off. The skies did not long remain untroubled, however, for he was back the next morning, and again, in answer to the loons' summons I drove him off, I don't know how much of a threat he was to them because all waterfowl react with fright if a large bird with a short neck (the length of the neck seems to be what they go by) flies over them.

One morning a delegation of visiting loons appeared on the pond, and this caused a lot of excitement among the local residents. They enjoyed a regular beanfeast, running on the water as if competing with each other, dipping bills convivially one minute, mocking and jeering each other the next. The parents lured the strangers well away from their young, but whether they constituted a real threat or were being used for drill purposes, I couldn't decide, as the parents called out almost continually to their off-spring to remain hidden. Young loons, like their parents, can keep very low in the water when they want to, and this they did until the strangers departed and the older birds gave the all-clear signal.

As the young loons grew bigger and less vulnerable, the parents, who seemed to find family life somewhat confining to their freedom-loving and solitary natures, encouraged them to fend for themselves, going off (perhaps for a change of scene as well as to find better fishing waters) for longer and longer stretches of time.

We were returning to camp one evening when my companion broke the even stroke of his paddle. "Listen! What was that?" he asked.

The sun had already set but there were a few bright bars in the western sky. As I listened to the plaintive sound I was suddenly transported back to another night, several years earlier, when we had followed the same sound in the darkness and fog. Now I discovered that it was being made by the young loons, whose parents had gone off somewhere and left them. Darkness was coming on, and, surrounded by enemies, they were lonely and frightened and probably hungry, too, and they were *mewing like kittens*.

One night when their parents seemed to have gone off, we had the first severe thunderstorm of the season and it was a humdinger. The lightning flashed almost continually, illuminating the pond one moment, plunging it into complete darkness the next. It was followed by explosive, earth-shaking crashes of thunder, and the wind came in angry squalls which stirred the lit-tle pond into whitecaps. Big trees at opposite ends of the pond were struck with a rending and splintering of wood, as their trunks were blasted into kindling.

The rain fell at last, in such torrents that by morning the water in the pond had risen five inches.

I was distressed when I thought of the young loons out there alone in that tempest. I could imagine that for young animals that had never ex-perienced a storm, and especially for those that had to spend the night un-protected on the water, it must have been terrifying.

It was barely daylight when I went down and stood at the water's edge. There was a peculiar orange glow in the sky and on the fog.

The young loons swam in toward the landing looking like a couple of whipped puppies. It was evident that their fears had been deeply stirred. I spoke to them gently, and with beguiling trust they came in closer than they ever had before. As I talked, they gave me close attention (young loons' eyes are brown, not red), with that wonderful responsiveness all birds, even the wildest, show, and for a few moments, at least, we were fully in tune with each other in one of the memorably happy moments of that summer.

Once it began to rain, it didn't seem to know when to stop, and one day, when the pond was hobnailed with rain drops, I was watching the young loons' not very successful efforts at fishing, when my attention was drawn to a wedge-shaped stick poking up out of the water. I had looked at this shoreline so many times that every stub and stick and log was etched on my memory as on a film, and my eyes picked that stick out at once from all the others. I kept staring at it, but not until it submerged and then reappeared did I realize I was seeing the wicked-looking head of a big turtle.

I was amazed and alarmed as I watched the ill-favored reptile, which looked as though it had come up out of some ancient weed bed of the past, to see with what stealth it stalked the young loons. All the other turtles I had seen up until now were torpid creatures, sunning themselves on logs, descending to the dark muddy depths at the slightest warning of danger, but there was nothing sluggish about *this* one.

Now and then it raised itself a little to bring its intended prey within better focus, bringing the top of its gray-green shell (the size of the average dishpan) above water.

I was horrified when I realized what its intentions were, and I asked my companion to load his old shotgun and see whether he could prevent its intended butchery.

The young loons didn't notice it, with no parents to warn them, but swam in closer and closer, and I had never longed so for the speech of a loon. At sight of us moving about on shore the turtle went under, seeming to suspect that our intentions were no more honorable than its own.

After about fifteen minutes, during which time the rain gently fell upon us, it surfaced again, somewhat nearer the loons, but too far for a good shot, so we pushed off in the canoe. This seemed to decide the turtle that if it remained where it was, its goose was about to be cooked, and things ended inconclusively with its descending to the muddy depths once more.

The next morning I looked for it and didn't see it, but happily the loons were still around. I'd almost forgotten about it when we were returning across the pond later that afternoon, and my companion pointed to a log on shore. There, sunning itself, one foot still in the water and looking twice as big out of water as in it, was the turtle. Its gray-green shell was the same color as the lichen on the log, only its rounded outline gave it away.

As silently as possible we hurried back to camp for the shotgun. We told each other it was unlikely it would still be there when we returned, but nevertheless we hurried back paddling as quietly as possible. And it *was* there.

I held the canoe steady, or tried to, while my companion tried to face the turtle so he could shoot. Finally I saw his finger tighten on the trigger but just then there was a little splash as the turtle slipped off into the water! The killer was still abroad and would be until the water became too cold for him, unless we were lucky enough to meet him again with a gun in our hands.

I looked for it many times in the days that followed, always hoping to be able to stop its deadly game of hide and seek before it ended in tragedy. I didn't see it again, however, until another warm, rainy day when the pond was, as before, pricked with raindrops. (Was it counting on the disturbance on the surface of the water to help conceal it?) Only after careful search with the binocular did I find it, for it had come up close to the far end of a log a hundred feet from shore where it rested with only its head out of water.

Again the young loons were swimming about alone, and what was even more disturbing, my companion had gone off in the canoe and I was stranded on shore. The turtle was too far out for me to take a shot at it.

It was midmorning and the young loons were not fishing, just playing around aimlessly as they sometimes did, waiting for their wings to grow strong enough for them to join their parents in flight. The older birds had probably been back earlier to feed them.

They continued to swim toward the turtle which was lurking under the end of the log. I tried throwing sticks in the water, but the young loons only looked surprised at such hostility and hardly changed their course. The turtle was too busy craftily maneuvering and watching the young birds to pay any attention to me. Perhaps he knew he was too far out for me to reach him.

Closer and closer the young loons swam. I hurried along the shore, picking up a couple of stones and throwing them toward the log. I was gratified to see the tip of the turtle's nose disappear. But then, alarmingly, a few seconds later, so did one of the loons. Sometimes, even when they weren't fishing, they would dive under an outjutting log and come up on the other side rather than swim around it. I didn't know, now, whether that was what happened or whether the turtle had clamped its jaws onto one of its legs and pulled it under.

The other loon changed its course and began swimming out into the middle of the pond, looking back over its shoulder from time to time. I watched and watched with growing anxiety for the reappearnce of the first, and when it didn't surface I kept telling myself that it had swum a long way under water and come up beyond the curve in the shoreline. Both young birds had come unscathed through so many dangers, I suppose I had begun to believe them almost invulnerable.

Had it been a lesser breed of bird I'd have given up looking for it sooner than I did. Finally, though, I had sadly to accept the fact that there would be only one young loon this year (if his luck held) to join the fall migration.

Right up until the first week in October I saw one or another of the parents return to see how their remaining offspring was faring. Apparently until they are able to fly (and perhaps for some time afterward) the parents have a feeling of responsibility toward their young. Anyway, when the loonlet followed its parent around and mewed and teased to be fed, the older loons still fed it.

Like all waterfowl that migrate, our young loon grew remarkably fast. It was still brown, and it did not, except for its bill which was growing long and sharp, much resemble a loon. It would not grow its handsome black-and-white plumage until it was at least two years old, and it would lose it again each winter.

Now, when it hung around camp it gave evidence of being almost as hungry for companionship as it was for food. Like all animals, it lived entirely in the present moment and it had no way of knowing it would not be grounded here for the rest of its life. When I called to it, it hunched its shoulders up around its ears and looked back at me almost coyly, rising on the water and flapping its wings in a deliberate, pleased kind of way at being noticed. Was it possible it would survive to return to the pond another year? I asked myself. Or would it succumb to a danger greater than any it had faced so far, once it took to the air? Watching, I felt the sorrow I often felt for all things tameless and free that live short lives.

Then, one windless morning in late fall, when the air around the pond was spiced with the odor of fallen leaves, wild aster, and ripening cattails and there was a soft, lilac haze on the distant hills, I saw what I think few persons have the luck to see. I was sitting on the shore, regretting that soon, now, we should have to leave the pond, when I saw a true conquest of space as my young loon took to the air for the first time.

For weeks it had been running on the water, as all loons must to take off, fanning the air with its narrow wings, never quite able, or perhaps not daring, to trust itself to the air, yet eager to follow the others. But this morning when it revved its propellers, it found itself suddenly airborne. It was not very high, it is true, but its feet were no longer dragging in the water.

Its uncertain flight took it around and around in a widening circle, back curved, neck drooping, big feet trailing out behind. Each circle took it a little farther above the pond, a little higher in the air, above the woods and water, higher and still higher, all the earth beneath it. It looked like a duck flying. Suddenly, from a full heart, its voice rang out clear and wild and joyous.

When it flew over me I called to it, and it answered in the same triumphant voice, though up until today when it had tried to call like a mature loon it had succeeded only in making what sounded like a shriek of rage, startling even to itself. It wasn't flying easily, but it was making up in intensity for what it lacked in skill. It reminded me of when I learned to skate, how I leaned forward on the wind, skating faster and faster, for fear that if I slowed down I should fall.

It circled the pond around and around, swinging joyously between earth and sky, then it began coming down, not without fear and a sharp cry of distress at the awfulness of having to descend from such a dizzying height on its narrow wings, dropping, plunging, sliding on its breast, until it pulled its feet under it in an awkward, three-point loon landing.

The next day when I looked for it, it was gone, its long journey into the unknown begun—and I and the pond were the lonelier for it.

NIGHT SONG

I sat alone before my campfire one evening, watching as the sunset colors deepened to purple, the sky slowly darkened, and the stars came out. A deep peace lay over the woods and waters.

Gradually the wilderness around me merged into the blue of night. There was no sound save the crackle of my fire as the flames blazed around the birch and cedar logs.

The moon came up behind the black trees to the east, and the wilderness stood forth, vast, mysterious, still. All at once the silence and the solitude were touched by wild music, thin as air, the faraway gabbling of geese flying at night.

Presently I caught sight of them as they streamed across the face of the moon, the high, excited clamor of their voices tingling through the night, and suddenly I saw, in one of those rare moments of insight, what it means to be wild and free. As they went over me, I was there with them, passing over the moonlit countryside, glorying with them in their strong-hearted journeying, exulting in its joy and splendor.

The haunting voices grew fainter and faded in distance, but I sat on, stirred by a memory of something beautiful and ancient and now lost—a forgotten freedom we must all once have shared with other wild things, which only they and the wilderness can still recall to us, so that life becomes again, for a time, the wonderful, sometimes frightening, but fiercely joyous adventure it was intended to be.

❧

THE BEARS OF FAT FISH POND

Soon after we had moved into camp on Fat Fish Pond I was looking out the window of the cabin, one evening, watching a doe browsing on the hillside when I saw her raise her head and lay her ears back as though listening to something behind her. Suddenly, not liking what she heard, she began moving off quickly and furtively.

A little later, I again looked out the window and this time I was startled by a big black object moving about among the greenery. With some alarm I saw that it was a bear.

There was an enormous, weathered log lying on the hillside sloping directly toward the cabin. I glanced toward it, and my heart jumped. Three more bears were coming down it!

When I got over my surprise, I realized I was looking at an old bear and her three cubs, now more than half grown and almost as tall as she was.

We had begun using a hole under the roots of the big fallen pine as a garbage pit, and it was to this they were going. After having been fed by the lumberjacks at a camp about five miles away, they now craved more civilized food. After my first feeling of fear had passed, I became absorbed in watching them.

One of the young bears found something wrapped in paper, and it jumped back onto the log, looking like a huge dog carrying a folded newspaper in its mouth. Since I had always thought of bears as slow and ponderous creatures, it was disquieting to see with what ease they jumped up onto the fallen trunk, a good three feet from the ground.

Good-naturedly, the young bear shared what it had found with the others. They were completely absorbed in what they were doing, and the mother stood back as though on guard, and watched. I was surprised to find what a close-knit family they seemed to be. I hadn't expected them to be so amiable among themselves, either, or so capable of expressing their enjoyment.

The next morning, while I was cooking pancakes, knowing what a keen sense of smell bears have, I kept looking out the window, and sure enough, what I expected happened. I saw one of the cubs jump onto the log. Abruptly, out of a clump of spruce, the mother appeared. She was limping, and I saw that she had lost a forepaw. She stopped and shook herself like a dog and water flew from her fur in all directions.

Suddenly I felt that I wanted to know more about these big animals, usually dismissed as "brutes." The textbooks were provokingly vague, saying only that they were nomads, making temporary dens under roots or in caves or holes in hillsides when cold weather set in, living mostly on berries, acorns, beechnuts, roots, honey, ants and their grubs, as well as mice and other small animals. There were known instances of bears having attacked people, but (except for captive bears) only when wounded or surprised, or in defense of their young. Nobody seemed to have interested himself in the mental and emotional lives of bears, nor in the part they played as individuals in the community of living things. I had made friends with wild deer, coons, squirrels, skunks, loons, ducks, all in their natural surroundings, free to come and go as they pleased. What I wondered, would a bear be like if one could study *him* in his natural surroundings? I decided to find out.

"You'll find out a lot more than you want to, if you're not careful," Mr. Rice warned me.

But I couldn't quite bring myself to believe him. Just how dangerous were the bears, anyway? I wondered.

The next time one appeared, it was about four o'clock of a still afternoon. I looked out the window and saw him on the pine log (which we were beginning to call the "bear log" since we never knew when we'd look out and see one there) and he was watching the pen behind the cabin in which we had a few ducks. This would be a good time to find out.

Before Mr. Rice could protest, I stepped outside. There was great individuality in the appearance of the different bears, I was learning, and this one, tall and slim, was not one I had seen before. I took several steps toward him and he pricked up his ears and stared at me inquisitively. He looked so knowing that I spoke to him familiarly, pointing to the ducklings in the pen shaking my head and saying, No, no, he could not have them, they were mine. Then I pointed my finger at him and ordered him sternly to be off.

He squinted nearsightedly and regarded me with close attention, and some surprise, as I talked. He didn't look a bit threatening, only curious.

"Go on! Be off!" I ordered emphatically, with gestures.

It was my turn to be surprised. He hung his head almost shyly, as if to say, "Nobody likes bears," then slowly turned and jumped down from the log and went off! Clearly he had understood by my voice and gestures what I meant to convey to him, and it was exciting to find how easily I could communicate with these big, potentially dangerous animals.

"I want to learn more about them," I told Mr. Rice. "I think I'll make friends with them."

"You'll only be asking for trouble if you do!" He warned. "A half-tamed bear's nothing to fool around with."

I knew what he had in mind. Our wood's privy was a good hundred and fifty feet from the cabin, along a narrow, wooded trail on which it would have been difficult to see a bear after dark. This thought often disturbed me, too, because the bears kept to the trail, and I didn't like to think what would happen if we stepped too close to one and frightened it. But the little I knew about them only made me want to know a lot more about "he who walks like a man."

One of the woodsmen who worked in the park told me the bears were not traveling around as much because they were feasting on the big suckers the men trapped in the trout streams and threw out on the bank. Suckers are a mass of small bones, and humans spurn them, but the bears welcome them eagerly, which showed how hungry they were at this time of year, before the berries and cherries were ripe.

One evening, soon after this when I had rather forgotten about them, I unexpectedly came face to face with the biggest bear I had seen yet. It must have weighed all of five hundred pounds. It stood its ground fearlessly, looking me right in the eye. I had never before been this close to a bear. I could actually *smell* it! I was unprepared for its bigness and its glossy blackness and its magnificently bold bearing, verging almost on the contemptuous. I had the feeling of enormous power barely held in check as we stood facing each other, and again I was struck by its look of intelligence. Here was a chance to communicate with one if there was ever going to be, but for some reason the desire to do so suddenly left me, and all I felt was an overpowering desire to be elsewhere.

As though in the presence of royalty, I began backing away; then, instinctively feeling I must not run, I turned and walked quickly to the cabin and called Mr. Rice through the open window.

The bear showed no signs of hostility, it simply stood and watched us and when it had watched us as long as it wanted to, it began slowly climbing the hillside. Upon reaching the top, it turned and looked back at us, and again, now that it was a safe distance away, I regretted not having made some sort of friendly overture toward it.

One morning, after the bears had begun coming around again for some time, I saw the mother, who now had two small cubs in addition to her own three half-grown ones. We learned later that she had adopted the two little bears after their mother was shot at a village garbage dump. There is less and less room left in the world for these big animals, which, like so much of our wildlife, are fast losing their battle against civilization.

It was sheer nobility on the mother bear's part to adopt the cubs; it is no small problem to raise a family of boisterous, irresponsible cubs.

Aside from the problem of food, the mother must keep the young out of reach of the father and all other big bears, which might kill them if they got in their way. The first lesson she teaches them is to climb, for only in the branches of some big trees are they safe.

When I stepped out of the cabin, she must have given this signal, now, for the cubs immediately went up in the trees, one of them squealing in fright. I wished I had something to give them, but our groceries had to be brought such a long way, I seldom had anything to spare.

It took a lot of food to nourish their big frames, and at this time, before the berries were ripe, they became desperately hungry. I hung fly traps on the trees baited with rotten fish, to keep the flies away from the unscreened cabin, and they wrenched the metal tops off the jars as if they were tin foil and ate the fish.

Once a week our mail and groceries were left in a wooden box on the far side of the pond. It did not take the bears long to find this out, and the day our groceries were delivered it became something of a sporting contest to see who got there first, we or the bears.

Perhaps the sight of other animals around gave them a feeling of confidence. One morning when I heard a mother duck with a brood of newly hatched ducklings vigorously protesting that something was not as it should be, I went out and looked at the hillside.

At first I saw nothing unusual, so I turned my head to look the other way and saw a bear lolling on the ground. He had just done away with one of my fly traps, and he was half sitting, half lying, watching the duck pen, for bears, like many other animals, are very curious. He raised his ears when I spoke to him, and they looked almost as big, although not the same shape, as a deer's.

When he got to his feet I saw that he was not a very big bear, really. He had a slim body and long legs, and he was limping. He began coming slowly down the hillside, and I stood my ground. When he went over a log I saw that he was dragging his right hind leg. People were always taking shots at the bears to drive them off, if they became too friendly. One bad thing about feeding them was that they soon lost all desire to find food for themselves.

By now the mother duck had worked herself into a state. She flew up onto the top of a cage, and her babies huddled in a frightened group below her. The bear watched them with interest for a while. What was going on in his mind? When he turned to look at me I was again struck by the position of his ears, his carriage, even a certain facial expression, which all showed the greatest alertness and intelligence.

Perhaps the mother duck's noise disconcerted him, however, because presently he went limping off up the hillside and out of sight.

Gradually the bears grew bolder and bolder. There was a kind of electric feeling in the air whenever one was around, shared by the deer (who left hurriedly), ducks, and geese, and even humans. As for myself, I was constantly torn between my desire to become better acquainted with them and my uncertainty of what they might be driven to do when they were so pinched for food; a bear's behavior is always unpredictable. The knowledge that they were bigger and stronger than I stood as a barrier between us.

Just at dusk one evening toward midsummer, I was outside, bent over the steps, filling a kerosene lamp when some slight change in the rhythm around me caused me to turn and look uneasily behind me. At first I saw nothing. Then I was aware of a black shape, blacker than the shadows. A bear was standing motionless behind me in the little hollow. He was so close that I had actually looked over him for a second without seeing him.

Quickly I bounded up the steps into the cabin. I called to Mr. Rice, and together we watched him out the open window. There was something very disquieting about the still way in which he stood regarding us. What was going on in his mind? Was he friendly or unfriendly, or merely curious? Would we dare to find out? Could we risk trifling with an animal that outweighed us by a couple of hundred pounds?

"By George, this has gone far enough, my companion said, making up his mind. He went over and took his shotgun down from the log wall. "Guess I'll have to scare him a little." To my regret, he loaded the old gun with fine shot. The bear watched fearlessly as he stuck the long barrel out the window, aimed at a small spruce beside him, and fired.

With the speed of an express train the bear bounded away over logs and through thick underbrush and disappeared into the woods.

And now comes the strangest part of my story. Although the bears had been appearing sometimes daily, and there were known to be at least twelve bears in the neighborhood, we never saw another bear that season!

I have talked about this with guides and woodsmen who are acquainted with bears, and although they have different theories about what happened, all of them agree on one remarkable thing—that bears have some way of communicating with each other. Some point to marks left by a bear on a tree whose bark has been scratched and torn some height from the ground. A bear, passing one of these trees, will stop and examine it, then stand on its hind legs, and, reaching as high it can, will gnaw and scratch the bark before going on. It has been suggested by some observers that bears have some sign language of their own, although others declare that the bear is just measuring his height against that of passing bears. Still others point to the bears' ability to vocalize or imply that they are capable of communicating on a level we know nothing about. None of these theories satisfied me.

Could there be, I wondered, such a thing as an *odor* of fear? If the ant, in its excitement at finding food, can lay down a scent trail for other ants to follow, why couldn't a bear, in its fright, leave a scent that would warn other bears away? Aren't dogs able to recognize the odor of fear in people?

Strong and unexpected support was lent my theory a few months later when I stood before the cage of a trapped brush wolf, a beautiful wild animal with a golden coat and yellow eyes.

"Smell him?" the trapper asked, when he came up.

"No," I said. I didn't smell anything.

"Well, I guess he's not afraid of you, then. But when he's afraid, or when someone he doesn't like comes near him, he smells worse than a skunk. Phew!"

Then there is such a thing as an odor of fear, I thought, watching the captive animal. Was it some such uric odor which had warned the bears that the cabin had become an unfriendly place for them, and had finally driven them away from Fat Fish Pond?

Alice Wolf Gilborn

Alice Wolf Gilborn

Raised on the outskirts of Denver, settled since 1972 in Blue
Mountain Lake, Gilborn exemplifies in her life and work some of the
common strands that weave through these mountain women's
writing. She may be best known as an editor, notably of the magazine
Blueline which she published, and of several Adirondack-related
pamphlets and books. Her editorial essays for *Blueline*, four of which
appear here, and several of her articles in *Adirondack Life*, reveal
Gilborn's concern with the creative life of mountain artists—sculptors, writers, painters, poets. In her prose and poetry one
finds the recurring idea of living against the land, creating a life that
is authentic, satisfying and survivable in an environment that constantly forces one to confront her own vulnerable humanity.

The first piece included here, "Of Birth and Blueline," suggests
the organic, visceral connection between living and writing which
gives form to her prose and touches on themes developed in her 1976
book about her family, *What Do You Do With A Kinkajou?* Gilborn
grew to girlhood in a bustle of animals fostered by her mother on the
five acre family farm in Colorado. Eventually the open spaces surrounding the farm were taken over by suburbia, a loss of freedom, independence and beauty which young Alice deplored. *Kinkajou* is
brimming with domestic detail of daily life among the mother's
horses, dogs, fowl and exotic creatures, including the kinkajou of the
title—a chaotic menagerie. Amid the jumble and affection, Alice
emerges as a child who didn't quite fit in, "the only girl sandwiched
between two brothers."[1] Underlying the girl's growing up is the colli-
sion between the conflicting personas of her maternal grandmother,
who represented gentility and ladylike ease, and her mother who,
with her robust lifestyle, was the outdoors-woman who was admittedly more attuned to animals than people. They were "three generations caught in a subtle web of love and obligation."[2] Gilborn recall-
ed the women walking together: "mother and daughter are almost
the same size: one pale, soft; the other brown, hard—both tough."[3]

Her memoir links Alice to a line of independent women who forged their own identities against the relative wildness of Colorado country.

Having had some paralysis from polio as a child, the girl strained to find the physical liberation and joy that her mother modeled for her while at the same time relishing the quiet, gentler ambience of the grandmother's life among linens and tea things. It was her grandmother, in fact, who sent Alice East to be educated at Wellesley College, an absence that generated loving letters full of life on the farm Willowcroft and the charge to write a book about it. While at college in Massachusetts, Gilborn often visited Au Sable Forks because returning to Colorado was too costly, and later she felt that her eventual move to the Adirondacks was inevitable since she already thought of them as her second home.[4] Perhaps Gilborn's impulse to write came from the grandmother, or from her mother, who felt so keenly her connection to her animals, particularly the horses, that she was "inspired to write airy poems . . . which she hid in her bureau drawer under her pajamas."[5] Gilborn knew from the fourth grade, while attending a private girl's school, that she wanted to write and began scribbling stories. Her own writing about her growing up creates a narrative focused on the life and death rhythms of country living where the unexpected and accidental dominate—flash floods, illness, injury, fierce weather—as though her days were continuously threatened by natural forces. In the epilogue which Gilborn is writing now, she chronicles what has happened to the land and people, the change and continuity.

It is curious that there is so little mention of the mountains and landscape in this autobiographical work. Most references are to the mountains as background, occasionally as hills against which, like the various adversities among her animals, her mother pits herself. It is this awareness of terrain as testing ground that pervades the Adirondack work of this writer, particularly two poems which are included here, "Portents" and "Alien Woods." That the mountains are crucial to her vision and sense of self is clear in an essay from 1981 titled "Landmarks." On flying back to Denver as an adult she mused:

> We had dropped in a cloud of dust. The mountains, my landmark, were
> gone. . . .I had just come from mountains—why was it necessary to salute

these? Were the Rockies still the calm eye of my own private storms? Which
were my home—the brown barren foothills backing Denver where I was
born or the green, water laced uplands of the central Adirondacks where I
lived? . . . .Mountains, no matter where, have always acted like magnets,
both attracting and repelling me. When we first settled in the Adirondacks
I felt submerged by forests, flattened by leaden clouds, bogged down in
mud. I longed to climb a high, scorched boulder and scan a treeless horizon
. . . .I was uneasy with the moist, frantic fecundity of the summer woods,
ferns uncurling overnight, thickets of which hopple, wine red trillium blooming in the shade. But when I returned to Colorado, the
mountains had lost their familiarity—they appeared to be protrusions
of the moon—parched, craggy, likeless. They made me thirsty just to
look at them.

   Yet extremes compress, and I hold the image of both ranges, east and
west, like a calm, close truth. I cannot imagine living where the land is flat
or absolutely dry. . . .Through the deep layered canyons of the Rockies,
across the blue tiered Adirondacks, the same currents swirl. The wind
above New York shifts just as suddenly as over Colorado. But under sun
and shadow and scudding clouds loom the mountains—silent, impervious,
centered in the midst of change.[6]

   The notion of centeredness is crucial to Gilborn's work, finding
firm ground for the rooting of a realized self. The mountains, east
and west, provide Gilborn with a place to grow, a constant presence
which, in contrast with the ephemeral nature of human life, provides
a measure of comfort in their constancy. In *Kinkajou* readers witness
the struggle of the girl to become a kind of woman her mother would
admire, connected to land and animals, elemental things. That girl,
after finally learning to milk a goat, noted, "By pleasing my mother's
animals, I knew I had been admitted to her world. I hoped, then, it
would never change."[7] In the Adirondack writing, one sees the
woman still negotiating a truce with the land and animals, bearing
her own daughter, and using her literary gifts to exlore the uneasy
relationship between artist and landscape. In the essays and poems
that follow, you will find a sense of landscape as eternal test, not a
benevolent or sublime presence, but a force against which women
and men endure and persevere, reclaiming and proclaiming
themselves.

OF BIRTH AND BLUELINE

Writing a story or a poem may be more inspirational than publishing a magazine, where the plot plods along unsensationally and the lines, in the form of inquiries or renewal notices, lack a certain lyricism. But whenever writing is issued to the world (or in many cases, to a couple of sympathetic friends), it involves the same creative process. Conception, incubation, birth —time honored terms borrowed from biology—have been used metaphorically to describe the evolution of everything from a novel to an advertisement. Anyone who has taken on the job of creator has felt the pangs of expectation, the effort of execution, and the exuberance or relief that follows the completion of his work. While I have labored over a single sentence with more fury than hope, more resignation than euphoria, I have always assumed that the mind begets much in the same way as the body. In the last year and a half I have proved my assumption to be true; producing a magazine is like producing a baby. Now, as I write, my infant daughter clutches a copy of BLUELINE, three issues old, and slowly hoists it to her moist, undiscriminating mouth.

Although BLUELINE predates Amanda, their histories have been intertwined almost from the beginning. BLUELINE'S gestation took place from April to August 1979, five hectic months shared by its staff writing letters, making calls, reading manuscripts, designing layout, typing, negotiating with the printer, proofreading, wooing subscribers. Our alternating bouts of uncertainty and anticipation were the more severe because of our collective inexperience in putting together a magazine, even a little one. On August 28th two heavy boxes of neatly packed BLUELINES arrived in Blue Mountain Lake from Brodock Press. Opening a box and drawing out the top copy, I felt simultaneously a surge of elation and a suspicious queasiness in my stomach. The next day I learned I was pregnant.

And so began my personal, pragmatic test of a very old metaphor. We would have to sell every copy of the magazine to guarantee its survival; nevertheless, as soon as the first issue was in the mail, we drafted plans for a second. We worried about attracting good Adirondack writing, spreading word of our existence, rising postal rates and other costs. We became hopeful as poems, stories and subscriptions trickled in, encouraged by complimentary reviews. My free time disappeared. I pushed the clutter across my desk, loosened my belt another notch and wondered what, at my age, I had let myself in for. Over forty, I was considered a risk. As a publisher I was a neophyte, destined to plunge the entire project into debt. Pregnant with my first child I was classified as an "elderly primapara." Somehow the adjective didn't fit the condition. In November we checked our distribution, and I learned at the same time the results of an amniocentesis done a month earlier. BLUELINE was sold out—and I was carrying a normal girl. After that, designations were forgotten.

Had Amanda arrived in April when expected, the third issue of BLUE-LINE might not have appeared at all; as it was, we were just able to make the final selection of poems and prose from our 130 submissions and prepare the copy for the printer. Driving the sixty miles to the hopsital in Glens Falls that mild night in early May, I was not, finally, thinking of the magazine at all. The night, I remember, smelled of hemlock; the moon, just full, streaked the road with pale light and shadows of rocks and trees. The air was still. The car felt as if it were floating outside of time; inert mountains massed against a black sky; even the dimly silvered Hudson, as we came down upon it at North River, seemed suspended. Inside, the cadenced pain began to rise precisely as a sonnet. At first I watched for deer, their eyes glowing a warning, then for the headlights of cars, but nothing broke the chiaroscuro of the road. Gradually I fell into darkness, self absorbed, certain of the work I had to do, anxious for the outcome. I was glad our daughter would be born on the day that followed such a night, in the shadows of the Adirondacks.

There are days when I think I have given birth to twins. The baby and the magazine constantly demand my time, and often they steal time from each other. I have learned that expectation is not the same as reality—I am pleased and always surprised when each issue of BLUELINE emerges with a personality of its own—it is not merely the sum of its parts. For an unknown reason, I envisioned Amanda with a shock of dark hair and brown eyes, or at least bearing the imprint of her mother, having occupied my body for nine months. What appeared was a bald but blonding version of my husband, with blue eyes and a double chin, slightly resembling Winston Churchill in profile. The biggest surprise, however, is that the baby and BLUELINE exist at all. Summarizing eighteen months of anxiety, discomfort and joy, they are still not finished, for they hold within them all the possibilities of growth and time. No longer do they belong to their creators but to themselves.

LIVING WITH THE ANIMALS

For eight years I kept a horse in the Adirondacks and rode by myself many hours through the woods. When she arrived from Colorado, the horse was suspicious of every shadow that lurked behind the trees. Her first day loose in the pasture she encountered several deer that had slipped under the wire fence and were ambling along a worn herd path. The reaction was immediate. Horse and deer flipped their tails over their backs and fled to opposite corners where they whirled and snorted at each other. Within a week, however, they were grazing quietly in the same field.

I soon discovered that the horse not only kept my feet out of the mud, she became a buffer between me and the wildlife I'd surprise from time to time. A red fox once chased a mouse under her hoofs, and a bear bobbed soundlessly up the trail not fifty yards ahead of her. From her back I'd spot a hawk or watch a pair of squirrels sparring in a white pine, and I'd try to mind my business and let the creatures attend to theirs. But I was going against my instincts. It was hard for me to resist plucking a fawn from its nest in the long grass for a better look. I intended no harm—motivated by curiosity rather than hunger, I was nevertheless aware of a predatory desire to inflict myself on a creature smaller and weaker than myself.

Man has imposed himself upon animals for centuries—he has hunted them, captured them, domesticated them, and taken their territory. He has enshrined them in his myths and literature: Pegasus, Moby Dick and Donald Duck all reflect man's varying attitudes toward animals, ranging from reverence and romance to ridicule. He has endowed them with his own emotions and characteristics, and while it may be generous to take animals so much to heart, it can also be corrupting. Witness the poets who succumb to the "pathetic fallacy" by attributing human feelings to animals and thus sentimentalizing their work. Or the owners who must cater to the gourmet tastes of their cats and the pet food companies.

In 1973 Congress passed the Endangered Species Act to help those species headed toward extinction by protecting their habitat from further encroachment by man and his projects. This year the bill is up for reauthorization by the Government. Interior Secretary James Watt has recommended that the ESA remain as is until October, 1983, pending changes that would improve it or, according to conservationists, drastically curb its effectiveness. During preliminary hearings in Washington, controversy has erupted over the expense and inconvenience of saving what some believe to be inferior forms of life. One senator even proposed that every species on earth but man could be considered expendable. His statement has given me pause.

Admittedly, our relationship with animals is not always easy—it can be highly selective and combative. We may wish for the survival of the species, but not all of them. We place our sentimental favorites like the giant panda or the sperm whale at the top of the preservation list, but we may not be so quick to add the three toed sloth or the hyena. We cringe at the clubbing of baby seals off Newfoundland, but who would object to the prospect of crushing the litters of millions of gray rats in New York City's sewers? We encourage sparrows, chickadees and other wild birds to gorge themselves on the seeds we provide each winter; now a farmer in South Bethlehem, New York, has been fined for poisoning over 2000 blackbirds that gorged themselves on his fall crop of corn. Scores of deer strip the blossoms from the apple orchards in upstate New York; a coyote, to some a symbol of wildness and isolation, skulks into a yard in a California suburb and carries off Mrs. Anderson's prize Siamese. After losing innumerable lambs to coyotes and eagles, sheep ranchers in Wyoming shoot to kill. Wild animals are neither moral nor sentimental and they do not operate by man's rules and expectations. Although they have taken some of their best meals at the expense of their reluctant human host, most of them could probably survive, even flourish, without his beneficence. But could we survive without them? Do we need the coyote, as well as the sheep? The sloth as well as the panda?

"I killed the last moose and trapped the last beaver that ever roamed the woods or dammed a stream in the lower Adirondack region," boasted Alvah Dunning in an interview printed by *The New York Sun*, June 6th, 1895. Dunning's attitude is typical of many of the Adirondack guides and hunters of the 19th century when the woods teemed with wildlife there for the taking. Dunning and his companions killed ". . . 100 moose one winter," and he himself shot ". . . eight monstrous big ones in five days," not to mention countless deer, bear and other wild game.

Yet we know today that hunting to the point of plunder was not responsible for the disappearance of moose from the Adirondacks. The cause has been traced to another forager, the white tailed deer which carried a brain disease harmless to themselves but fatal to the moose. Beaver, reintroduced to the Adirondacks, have made a healthy comeback. Dr. Rainer Brocke, director of the Adirondack Wilderness Fauna Program, in an article in *Adirondack Life* (March/April, 1982) writes about the problems and possibilities of the moose and other extirpated species such as the panther, lynx and golden eagle returning to the region. Brocke's program is "dedicated to C.H.D. Clarke's proposition that 'wildlife is more than anything the hallmark of quality' in a wilderness area." By extension, the absence of wildlife seriously diminishes the richness of man's experience in this area or any other.

This year I am without my horse, and during my walks I see far less wildlife than I did before. I'm more aware of my feet, the boggy earth, the devilish roots that crisscross the trail. On a day in November, after the seasonal birds have gone back and the first covering snow reveals the reassuring tracks of snowshoe hare and other creatures, the woods seem dreary and empty, with only the rustle of dry leaves and the cold creak of trees in the wind to give a suggestion of life. I wonder then, if every animal but man were expended, would these woods be worth walking in?

"I think I could turn and live with animals, they are so placid and self-contained," wrote Walt Whitman in "Song of Myself" (1855). "I stand and look at them long and long/They do not sweat and whine about their condition/They do not lie awake in the dark and weep for their sins/ . . . .Not one is dissatisfied . . . / . . . .Not one is respectable or industrious over the whole earth/So they show their relations to me and I accept them."

Whitman may never have encountered a sewer rat or a flock of starlings, but wisdom flows in his lines. It wouldn't hurt for certain denizens of Washington, D.C. to stand and look at the animals—long and long. They might decide that a snail darter is worth a dam. They might even discover room in the same pasture for the horse, the deer, and themselves as well.

OUT OF THE BLUE

They come out of the blue, two at a time, slicing the bright air in unison, so sudden and close that we stand stunned in the shattered calm of our afternoon as if a giant locomotive had just roared across the horizon. They come from bases outside the Blue Line, rockets on their wings, prong-nosed, twin tailed, A-10 attack planes slow for jets, built to sweep under enemy radar and deliver their lethal message to earth. The Adirondacks are their training ground, their mythical war zone. No matter how many times they come they transfix us with their beauty and power, but they leave behind a momentary sense of menace. If we had been lulled before by the quiet harmony of lakes, mountains and forests on a windless day, our peace is gone and the air now hums with dissonance.

In his book *The Machine in the Garden* (1964), Leo Marx explores in depth the intrusion of an alien technology into the realm of nature, or more exactly, man's ideal of nature. Marx begins with an example from Hawthorne's notebooks. Hawthorne has retreated to a hollow in the woods for the purpose of recording in minute detail the natural phenomena around him. In the midst of his close observations of leaves, twigs, the play of light and so forth, he is startled by the sharp whistle of a locomotive, immediately reminding him of the heat and bustle of cities, an intrusion of the commercial world and its machines into his solitude. His mood changes from one close to euphoria to melancholy. Nineteenth century writers and artists often used the railroad as a metaphor for progress, an emblem of power. Opposing them were those who viewed the "Iron Horse" with fear and skepticism.

Hawthorne and others, including Emerson and Thoreau, paid tribute to man's technological advancement, but they also saw it as a danger, an invasion of privacy and the natural, if idealized, order of things. In his story, "The Celestial Railroad," Hawthorne's train never gets beyond purgatory.

The Adirondacks in the latter part of the 19th century sported their own railroads which helped open up the region and encouraged the growth of industries such as mining and logging. Entrepreneur William Durant, anticipating great recreational development, built steamboat and rail lines in the central Adirondacks and made plans for extensions that would link widely scattered towns and villages by encompassing thousands of miles of wilderness. Durant's scheme failed, but progress had made its inroads. At the end of the century, however, with the establishment of the Forest Preserve by the state of New York in 1885, a counterforce emerged: the recognition of wilderness as a commodity in itself which must be protected by law from future exploitation. A provision in the Constitution of 1895 proclaimed state-owned lands throughout the Adirondacks to be held "Forever Wild."

Almost 100 years later parts of the Adirondack Park as it is known today are still forever wild, but they bear the scars of man's intrusions. Signs of this technology are everywhere: automobiles rip across mountain highways, snowmobiles spin through woods on a web of trails, seaplanes drop hunters and fishermen into hidden lakes and ponds. Even in the core of the Adirondacks clouds filled with chemical particles from midwest factories rain acid on the water and the land.

Yet people continue to come here, drawn by their dreams of wilderness, not to exploit it but to find some necessary link between the natural world and themselves. Some want recreation in all senses of the word; others want to test themselves in the wild; still others are driven by the age old need to withdraw from the complexities of society and return to a simpler, Arcadian way of life. Paradoxically, the less spoiled a scenic area is, the more people wish to retreat to it, thereby diminishing its uniqueness. The Adirondacks has its share of escapees from New York City and other civilized centers espousing the same pastoral ideals that inspired the poet Virgil centuries ago.

Living in a region whose value is determined by how much of its wilderness is preserved, we are especially aware of the dichotomy between the primitive virtues of the past and the technological achievements of the present. To what degree are the two compatible? We drive our cars to trailheads and ride neoprene rafts down wild rivers. The French aviator Antoine de Exupéry believed that the machine, the airplane in particular, would eventually unite all mankind by annihilating time and space. For him, the airplane was a means to an end, a mechanical tool in the service of humanity's spiritual quest to understand one another and join together for the common weal. As for the natural world, "the machine does not isolate man from the great problems of nature, but plunges him more deeply into them," wrote Satin Exupéry in the 1930s. Fifty years and several wars later we can marvel more than ever at the genius and sophistication of technology, but its service to mankind may not be quite what Saint Exupéry envisioned. If man's beautiful machine spells destruction with its contrail, do we want it plunging into our garden?

The Adirondacks may fall short of Eden, yet it is here in this forest preserve that men have a chance to make a covenant with nature and to find that hollow in the woods so necessary to the human spirit. Perhaps it is not possible in the 20th century to shed all the crustations of civilization, to die down to the root, as Thoreau put it, to revive again in a simpler form. But because a majority of legislators in 1885 took a conservative view of progress, we have a country in which to try. The red trillium by the trail in spring, the ripple of flame across the hills in autumn, the rosy glow on the mountain on a winter afternoon are brief and seasonal, but we don't need much to remind us that we live at the hub of the great wheel of nature turning as it has done for millions of years. Until the jets fly over.

THE PROVING GROUNDS

Not long ago my young daughter selected me to read her a bedtime story about the solar system in her new children's encyclopedia. I pointed out the earth, which occupied front page center, and its important orbit around a huge and fiery sun. On the next page, however, the sun was reduced to the status of a star no larger than a white dot in a great swath of stars called the Milky Way Galaxy. The galaxy itself had shrunk to an indistinct white whorl on the following page, one among millions, the book cheerfully informed me.

I pondered the implications of this for about ten seconds. If the sun was just a pinprick of light in the scheme of things, then the earth was microscopic and I was infinitesimal. Zero, in fact. The few cubic feet of space my body filled counted as nothing. I continued staring at the bouquet of galaxies until my daughter poked me. I sighed. This sort of thinking could lead to insomnia. But then again, it had possibilities. What if I didn't exist?

If I didn't, I wouldn't have to read bedtime stories. I wouldn't have to have a nice day. There'd be no need to take charge of myself or take a course in assertiveness training or behave like Jane Fonda. Best of all, I could sit serenely in my living room and gaze at Blue Mountain without a twinge of guilt because I hadn't climbed it in ten years. If I didn't exist, I could live happily in the Adirondacks without ever having to challenge nature in order to prove myself.

I have nothing but admiration, on the other hand, for those who come here each year to do just that. They congregate at the trailheads, their worldly possessions roped to a frame on their backs so that from the rear they look like ladders wearing boots. Sometimes one overturns and lies stranded in the road. You know they have hiked a long way or are preparing to hike a long way, but you don't ask them why because part of proving yourself is to do it and not talk about it except to yourself. That you can do endlessly. Stories I read are full of interior monologues on the how-to's of proving yourself. It seems you first get in touch with nature, then you overcome it, then you get in touch with yourself, and at last you find your roots. Unfortunately, my roots extend only as far as the first comfortable chair.

Once I asked a backpacker why he wanted to snowshoe up a mountain in the dead of winter with a windchill of minus 30° and risk a broken neck skiing down. I received a look of utter contempt. Now I hold my tongue when muscular young men and athletic gray haired ladies tell me they've been to the top of all forty-nine of the Adirondack's highest peaks or paddled 100 miles through rain, sleet, wind, and clouds of biting insects. They've tested themselves against the elements and I have not, even though I live smack in the middle of the proving grounds. Because I'm a woman, I feel especially guilty; my duty is to prove myself so I can tell all the men about it. For instance, I could build a log cabin in the woods, live in it a winter, then write a book about my experience in the wilderness. Or I could build a lot of log cabins and sell them. But I suppose that would be sacrificing character for quantity.

Every summer joggers and bikers labor up Blue Mountain Hill, and by their knotted muscles and grimacing faces, I know they are quietly proving themselves. Every fall early bear hunters loudly prove themselves at the town dump and at the Bear Trap Bar. Once I rafted through the Hudson River Gorge when the waves looked like the broadside of a bus, but that only proved my luck was good and I was eligible to survive that day. When we first moved to the Adirondacks, we bought a canoe in anticipation of conquering numerous large lakes, including Raquette, but the canoe had all the hydrodynamics of a bathtub, and despite our efforts stalled in the slightest headwind. So we bought a motor for it. I should have realized then that there was small hope of my ever rising to nature's challenge when I could so willingly trade a paddler for a 3 hsp engine.

After a few moments of heavy silence my daughter instructed me to forget the universe and move on to insects. Once more my perspective went into shock. From an ant's point of view, I not only existed, I was an immense mound of flesh capable of creating a colossal disturbance. With my every step a shudder passed through the anthill. Being a giant, I was well equipped to confront whatever nature had to offer, even ants. Being human, I'd have to prove myself after all. I sighed. I could ease into it slowly by taking a walk in the woods during hunting season. But I'd rather do something more appropriate to my size, something gigantically human, like digging through the rubble of an earthquake for eight days straight and bringing forth, alive, a newborn baby. That would be proof to last a lifetime.

PORTENTS

Something in the chain was broken
the bird bumping on the window
like a moth or night born thing
frantic for the inside light —
no owl nor hawk but a warbler
numb from fright in a dark land.
Yet days ago the geese came gabbling
down miles of icy air sixty
straight strung from tail to tip
hooked and certain of their aim.
Since then children found
in the woods the skeleton
of a dog, around its brittle
neck a rope, one end knotted
in the brush. Hunters stalking
bear stumbled on a plane
crashed twenty years ago,
a rusted husk, but of a body
not a trace, not a bone.
Squirrels black as pitch seized
the hemlock; the air changed.
Last night bird, bat, slapped
against the wall and froze.

There was a time when all things
strange seemed portents, when
mousing owls killed falcons,
horses broke their stalls
attacked their masters, Birnam
wood uprooted, crept to Dunsinane.
Bird, beast, forest mirrored
man's transgressions; nothing
then was accident.
Yet better to believe that ancient
order, in nature signalling some
massive wrong, than a world gone
gray and careless — where men
and dogs die undiscovered, birds beat
their futile lives against a glass.

BIRDS

They struck with brief beating wings
against the fender; something
shuddered. I kept going not
daring to brake. In these mountains
winter roads are packed with snow,
on top, sand, and birds flock down
to glut their craws with grit.
Grosbeaks, sparrows, crows,
grounded, slow to sense
the tremor in the frost,
wheels dense looming,
rise with effort,
too late.

There was a jet that sucked into
its engines wild swans passing
south, a fatal confluence.

In that glacial brilliance
all flight stopped, struck
earthwards, blazing steel
and feathers. Accident.
Justice. Death by any
name. I keep going
certain of it. Behind
me the road, the snow,
the corpses on
the sand.

ALIEN WOODS

Bone weak, against the freshened earth
he would lie down, but feared his
sleeping. Leaves clawed his face;
the bright wet grass sprung nails.
Lifting his ankles high he kept on
through thick and tangled lavender
of flowers, gasped for other air,
shuddered at the carcass of a hare,
the young crows that sucked its milky
eyes. A cone of streaming ants
he crumbled without a curse. Yet
in another place and time he might
have made a worse Thoreau. Sensitized,
his forking vision probed the small
dark clusters of the woods, fingers
stabbed the belly of a log, beaded
with grubs. Shiny and exposed
the beetles ran. In the woods his
nerves were singing, like gnats
singing, of death and too much life.
He turned away, city bound. Among
the still and fractured faces of his
humankind he would begin to sleep.

TRANSIT

Today he brings me wildflowers
with tenderness erratic as the first
red that flags the August maples.
His gift recalls an old gesture,
youth to parent, man to woman
yet he bears the flowers like a child,
some uprooted, petals dropped
in transit, the whole unedited
bouquet plunged in a screw top jar.

I gaze through the glass at aquatic
undergrowth, hope for a fish
to part the leaves but think again
of trees laden in the torpid air
their hard green cargo dragging
at the branch. My son swims out
to shake them of apples like last
winter's snow; all spring skywards.
How much weather it will take
for them to redden, drop and die.

WHEN THE ICE GOES OUT

Old winter dies they say
black and brittle as ice on a jig
sawed lake splitting up in May.
In March it moved when we
walked on it, disorder foretold
by a deep and distant boom.

Old winter goes they say
with the first trout lily
blooming by a sodden trail in limb
locked woods. Widow makers brace
each other. When the buds come we can
better tell the living from the dead.

Streams crawl out from snowbanks,
fill up flows, go boiling down
the Hudson; stones long brooded
by frost hatch in the mud.
Winter's done they say.   ·
When overnight the ice goes
out and the lake breaks shiny
sleek as a peeled snake, we celebrate.
Yet for a moment in your shrouded
eyes I see old winter living still.

EVENING AND EARLY SORROW

Always when I look at you   for Sally
I see the shadow of your son
upon your face. Eyes dark
as moth's wings, his smile
a sudden bend of light.
Turned ten you let him
ride his birthday with your
friend in that sleek bright
hunkered down machine pressing
the mountain road too fast
until the missed curve seemed
like flight, the car a comet
looping through the trees.
Later you knew. Sirens
you never heard shattered
your skull, flames gutted
your heart. Yet you stand

here, black eyes circling my
own boy with his big hands,
pants an inch above his ankles
wanting out, wanting to go
if only for an hour. There
is nothing we can save him
from. He runs toward the sun
while we wait, bracketed
by ghosts, in the slow dusk
of his leaving.

Jean Rikhoff

Jean Rikhoff

The second novel in Jean Rikhoff's trilogy of the North Country, *One of the Raymonds*, begins with a quotation from Thoreau's *Walden* as an epigraph:

> I went into the woods because I wanted to live deliberately, to front only
> the essential facts of life, and see if I could not learn what it had to teach,
> and not, when I came to die, discover that I had not lived.

With other writers represented in this collection, Rikhoff harkens back to the idea of immersion in Walden-like wilderness. Martha Reben was said to have briefly done for Weller Pond what Thoreau did for Walden; Anne LaBastille created a new Walden experience and reflected that in the tradition of Thoreau's narrative in her newest work, *Beyond Black Bear Lake*. Rikhoff uses the nineteenth century text as touchstone and emblem of her vision of nature in its wild state as a place to learn about oneself.

Rikhoff's quest is purposefully literary as well as personal. She began *Buttes Landing* with the notion of writing the Great American Novel, beginning with the saga of Odder Buttes settling in the Adirondacks and begetting a line of descendants who would mingle with the Raymond clan and spread the tough North Country character across the United States. Early on the author recognized the need for keeping such an American novel regional, that is, telling the story by centering it in different parts of the nation and moving her North Country characters through those regions but always keeping the family rooted in the mountains. Rikhoff's idea for the undertaking is expressed in the second book of the series, *One of the Raymonds*, when Mason Raymond speculates on the need for a uniquely American story.

> Imagine, Mason Raymond thought, even trying to explain to a class—any
> class—at a school a sunrise like this and men and dogs like this. They
> wouldn't understand just as once he hadn't. The teachers at the Academy

maybe didn't even know what being American meant. They thought it was acting like a well-bred Englishman. That was really what they were trying to teach their pupils: to be American Englishmen.

But Americans didn't talk like Englishmen. They didn't think like them or act like them. They weren't in any way like them at all. They were themselves—or lots of selves. Because the Americans Mason Raymond knew here at the Landing weren't like the Americans who lived in the mountains down South and he didn't think they were probably much like the Americans out West, they weren't like city or even town people. There were lots of Americas, maybe so many that it was impossible to grasp the whole and say "This is it" because it wasn't it, only a part of the whole; but there must be some way to bring all of it together, the farms and towns, his uncle's place, the Landing; and the big cities with their fancy houses and their terrible, poor towns, like Albany, or Schenectady, like New York; there must be a way to capture the North and South, the West, the mountain people and the ex-slaves, the farmers and the millworkers, all of them, and say, See, *this* is it.[1]

In all three of these works, firm North Country values inform the characters and plots. The stories span ten generations of Buttes and Raymonds as they hack out a life in the upstate wilderness and mix blood and destinies with the Indians who still cling to the land. The novels begin with a single man tramping over the upland wilderness until he finds the spot of earth he feels he can subdue and make his own, an inhospitable, lonely tract at the edge of fictional Federation Lake (Lake George). The remaining narratives take family members and an assortment of Adirondack characters south to North Carolina and in the third book, *The Sweetwater*, West through Missouri, Kansas, and Nebraska to Independence Rock, Wyoming, a place that in the year of the centennial, 1876, signified to them the spirit of self-sufficiency as thoroughly as did Thoreau's July 4 declaration of independence at Walden Pond.

Rikhoff has created taut narratives rich in the diversity and peculiarity that characterize North Country folk. Odder Buttes and Cobus, whose stories are excerpted here, are embodiments of the back-country ethos; Mason Raymond is better educated and more urbane. Odder and Cobus plunge deeply into the wilderness to find themselves; Mason enacts a mythic quest for understanding by leaving the dark wooded mountains and going into the larger world where he finds pain, degradation, death—and himself. *The Sweetwater*, like the two previous books, is about seeking the self. As

Mason Raymond and John Buttes make their way across the country, they find new images of the men they are, shedding the overlay of family and region to get at the elemental self. The ethical wilderness of the West, an analog to the terrestrial wilderness of the Adirondack mountains, provides the setting where they can confront the essential facts of their being.

Rikhoff's command of North Country character and narrative belies a consciousness that is intimately connected to the people and land of the Adirondack region but is in no way parochial. Indeed, Rikhoff, like most of the writers included here, came to the mountains as a young woman. Raised in Indianapolis, she attended a convent school until she was twelve. As soon as she could, she escaped the Midwest and life with an abusive father, attending college in Massachusetts at Mt. Holyoke. After receiving her undergraduate degree, she returned to Wesleyan (where she had relished being the only female student) and completed a master's degree. Immediately she left for Europe — "like Hemingway and Fitzgerald" — to teach and travel for seven years with her first husband. It was in Seville that she wrote her first book, *Dear Ones All* (1961) about her Hoosier family. Then followed *Voyage In, Voyage Out* (1963) and *Rites of Passage* (1966). Eventually she moved to Bolton Landing with her young daughter, married a local man, and subsequently spent twenty years on a farm along the New York-Vermont border, a time of interdependence with the land which she calls her "pioneer period." *Buttes Landing* appeared in 1973 and was chosen a Book of the Month Club alternate and optioned for a television movie before it appeared in paperback in 1975. *One of the Raymonds* attracted the same attention, and *The Sweetwater* followed. Rikhoff was then diverted from her plan to write an American saga by pressure from her editor to write an "obligatory woman's novel," *Where Were You in '76?* (1978). From 1954 to 1966 she had been editing *Quixote Review*, an anglo-american quarterly which she founded; her editorial interest and expertise led her to help found The Loft Press and publish *The Glens Falls Review* beginning in 1983. Currently she teaches at Adirondack Community College and is active in academic and literary pursuits while writing a new novel about Granville, New York. Her honors include receiving the Eugene Saxton Fellowship in creative writing, a National Endowment for the Humanities fellowship, and a State University of New York creative writing fellowship.

With her character Odder Buttes who believed that "People who like mountains were one breed; people who like valleys another" and that there was a vast difference in quality between "those who looked up into the unknown and those who squatted in the safe, flat places,"[2] Rikhoff is convinced that geography is crucial and that escaping to the Adirondacks got her away from the "flat minds" of the Midwest. Odder Buttes, also fleeing from the brutality of men in the Midwest, pits himself against the hills in a way that echoes the impulse to rape the land that pervaded the nineteenth century. In the excerpt from "Odder's Book" which follows, the title character strains against the mountains:

> He wasn't going to go through an ordeal like this without paying something back, and if the woods put him through it, then it was the woods he would pay back.
> A man with an axe could see to that.[3]

That tenacity born of desperation is what keeps Buttes on the land, rooted to the mountainside when others merely passed through on a binge of exploitation and curiosity. One of Rikhoff's abiding questions since settling in the region has been why people choose to live there, why they stay. It seems that they have made "an almost moral choice" to live and work where they can affirm themselves by enduring against the trials of weather and mountains. Though the mountain range in the first half of the nineteenth century was considered *man's* country by trappers, intellectuals, traders, and woodsmen, there are in Rikhoff's novels a number of beautifully realized female characters, women who are loved and respected by the rought wilderness men who chop and apportion the land and its goods while the women birth and build on it. There is little distinction between male and female values attached to the land, only the sense that there is a mythic female who inhabits that kind of wilderness, a womanhood embodied in Emily, Benji, and the Indians, women who have found identities for themselves outside the pantries and parlors of civilization.

Like her characters, Rikhoff believes that the point of living is risk-taking, pushing oneself against facts to find one's own grain. Used to pushing limits, Rikhoff has begun writing poetry; three of her pieces are included here. One, "Grieving the Garden of Eden," attests to the complicated religious shift that has occurred since her

Catholic girlhood. She now calls herself an atheist-existentialist and—like all the women included in this study—has found a new belief system for herself, one which puts forth courage as the prime virtue and activism as the prime responsibility. Pervading all Rikhoff's work, prose and poetry, is the will to risk seeking the self. Her characters, like Thoreau, live deliberately and essentially.

❦

In the beginning, when he came East over the mountains, Odder Buttes never thought of a lake. What he had in mind, coming over the Appalachians, was not water at all but mountains, a mountain farm, away from everyone, something so large that he could feel surrounded by the safety of space. What little money he had wouldn't buy much good land. Leastwise what others called good. But mountain land, land that was full of forest and scrub and rock, that was steep and hard for a man to go up and down, let alone take out trees, clear and plant, try to keep from going back to brush, that should come cheap. Nobody wanted woodland, nobody but Odder Buttes.

Valley people shunned the mountains because it was easier to till flat fields and because they believed that pine woods made for "weak soil." A man needed hard wood for "strong soil." Odder considered this a lot of nonsense; soil was soil. A man might wear it out, but trees couldn't, leaves didn't. People who like mountains were one breed; people who liked valleys another.

A man learned to make divisions all his life—earth, air; fire, water; love, hate; endless divisions that made up the oneness of being—why shouldn't he just as naturally make that kind of distinction between men?—those who fled, and those who fought; those who had, and those that didn't; those who looked up into the unknown and those who squatted in the safe, flat places.

Odder wouldn't have wanted valley land if it had been given to him. He had been wandering over flat country for years now—horse hand, hired hand, teamster, cradler, flailer, hogger, rope winder, joiner, foot peddler, even dowser, though he had never really had the gift for finding water; still he'd given it a try. Give anything a try once—there was another dimension you could make: those who needed new scenes and experiences same as they needed water and sleep and those that were afraid of the unexpected as if it was some kind of trap made to catch the unwary. A man who went soft and safe wasn't likely to expand himself, but he wasn't likely to have got in all the trouble Odder'd made for himself neither.

Something off balance in him maybe. Any time something came easy, he got suspicious. He had learned to distrust just about everything you could think of—women of course, most men, naturally the suspicious world around him, even himself.

Out where he'd been—Indiana, Ohio, Illinois, a part of Kentucky—the seasons came at you all in a rush, ended too abruptly, or hardly came and went at all in some places, there was just a monotonous regularity, a kind of permanent wavering climate that got on your nerves, told you, don't trust 'em. You put your corn in afore the first of May, you're gonna live to regret the day. Warm as August in April, cold as Kansas in August. What he had in mind was the kind of place where the seasons were pretty well portioned out, say about three months apiece, just enough time for a man to anticipate, appreciate, and then grow tired, start looking forward to a change; and the change would come. I'm goin' upstate New York, he had thought.

It was a decision that made no sense at all. He didn't know New York. He'd been born in New Jersey and lived there the first eight years of his life. He had impressions—vivid ones—of the old farm, but he didn't know the country farther north. His father had uprooted them all from New Jersey and moved them to Ohio a year after the Ordinance of 1787 opened the frontier and settlers streamed by flatboat, barge, or overland wagon, even on foot, toward the fabled fertile lands.

New Jersey had been flat. Ohio flatter. When he got older and moved on to Indiana, he began to believe, like the people of old, the whole world was flat. You keep walking, you just drop off the end. Men tried to tell him about mountains and he listened, but it was hard to believe what you hadn't seen, didn't know first-hand. But you made pictures. He had lots of pictures up there, in his mind. Bad business, them mountains, men said, you don't want to mess around with mountains 'less you're with a man knows his way around. You don't monkey with places like that, they said, unless you don't mind meetin' your Maker. *Bad* business, and what kind of life you goin' to have in a place like that? they would ask. No women 'less you count squaws, the men all cutthroatin' thieves, nuthin' but trouble and tribulations, more than one good man went into those woods and never come out, experienced men, too. Man, they said to one another, I'm never goin' back there no more. But as they said that, a kind of fire was kindled in their eyes, they seemed for a moment to *be* back and they were glad, it was a place they had never forgotten because there was *something* there.

What Odder wanted to find out was what that *something* was.

A man maybe could farm there? he would ask. You could maybe clear some of the land and—

Farm there? That's *woods*. People don't farm there. Even the Indians don't do more than pass through. That ain't settlin' land. It's only meant to be moved over. Hunt and fish some, all right. But farm? It's for the bear and rattlers.

But if you cleared out the trees, Odder persisted, you could farm then, couldn't you?

You clear out the trees, they'd just bolt back. That kind of place don't stay cleared. You gotta see that country to know what you're talking about.

But long years on the move had given Odder confidence. He thought he knew the worst there was to know about what could happen to a man. A lot of that knowledge came from personal experience, but he had survived, he was older and tougher, he didn't reckon there was much that could surprise him any more, or wreck him. Such things had come earlier and were over. He considered himself a man in balance now; he thought he understood the world and knew what it could do, and he figured he was big enough to whip some woods.

So he decided to go take a look for himself. It was March, springish; for Illinois and Indiana farmers the real beginning of the year, time for plowing up and getting ready for planting. He set out with enough money in his pocket to keep him going for quite a spell. When that ran out, he'd find work, he always did. He had been wild in his way, yes, but he wasn't wasted; he'd saved some money, a pretty good packet of it, and that had been put away with the bankers to keep safe. He wouldn't touch that. The bank money was going to buy his land, to get him a place of his own no one could ever take away from him, some place he could say was *his* and no one else's; a man needed yardage to make himself feel needed. Odder set a lot of store on being necessary. He got nervous when he could lay up and it made no difference, always tried to keep himself in situations where he had certain obligations every open hour of the day, he was *necessary*.

But there was a difference between doing duties other people put on you and erecting obligations of your own. He hadn't found other people that accommodating to his notions, his hankerings; he was always running up against someone who was trying to make him do something he didn't want and finding he had to do it to hold onto a job or get a woman or keep a situation soft and easy to live with. He wanted some say about himself, was sick and tired of other people holding power over him.

The way he began to figure, a man had to have a plan. A man without a plan just went hither and yon; nothing kept him in pitch. He wore himself

out in fretting and frittering. But a man with a plan, he had a direction he
was going and it gave his life form.

He had watched most of the men he knew marry and settle into thiev-
ing work that robbed them of their vitality and gave back little 'cept debts, a
parcel of children and a wife who tied more ropes around them. To Odder
that wasn't a life at all, it was some kind of bondage, the kind he'd thought
was over and done with when the days of indenture were finished; but there
were other kinds of debts and prisons men fell into and you had to watch all
the time one of them didn't reach out and nab you.

What he wanted was something just his own. A piece of earth just for
him to stand on. His sky. His place. But not flat. He had been a long time
figuring out everything—how much money he'd need, how he'd hike back
East—a horse was too costly and most likely would be no good at all in the
kind of country he had to cross—and then when he'd found what he wanted
and got a deed for the place, he'd need a stake—flour and salt, seeds, a cow
maybe, a man could get along on next to nothing if there was a reason for it
and he knew the effort was going toward something. Being poor didn't matter so long as you knew it wasn't permanent or without cause. He was a Jefferson man in that. Every man had a right to his chance, regardless; he held
with Jefferson that the country was based on the small farmer and the small
farmer wanted as little of government messing around with him as he could get.

A country was lucky, any time, to get men like Jefferson. Some people
might make fun of Jefferson's ways and be scandalized by his clothes, but
those were the people who had voted for Adams in 1800 and didn't matter
anyway. Jefferson knew what he was doing all right. Take the Louisiana Purchase: whoever controlled the Mississippi controlled the country. He had
been West in his wanderings and he *knew*. Jefferson had just been smart
enough to guess.

It took Odder some time to get back East. Whenever he got tired of
traveling, he would stop and work awhile and make a little money; then he
would pick up and take off again. He met a woman on the way that took up
more time than he liked, but while he was forgetting with the flesh, the
mountains hadn't seemed so important, another thing was on his mind;
then that other thing began to lose its interest and the vision of the mountains came back and at last the mountains were all that mattered, he was on
the move again. He had been traveling over easy country, the interior plains,
back through Ohio, and he didn't detour any out of his way to go back to
the family farm, he just kept going East. There wasn't anyone there he really
wanted to see and going home would have only meant counting up the
dead, reckoning at last with what had happened since he'd left. The way he
figured, he didn't have any family any more; he hadn't since the day he
walked off the place.

He crossed the Alleghenies and went up through the Finger Lakes and into the Mohawk Valley. That valley made a sick emptiness inside as he looked at the neat farms, thinking back to all the skirmishes and scalpings, the endless raids that had destroyed place after place, the people stubbornly hanging on, even though all they could do was watch helplessly from the forts as their houses and barns were burned, their livestock butchered, their crops put to the torch. A lot of those early settlers had been caught and tomahawked before the fort gun boomed the alarm that Indians were on the warpath again, and they had been cut down wherever they were — out haying, berrying, just walking up a road to their homes. He went quickly across the Mohawk Valley; it had been bought with blood and the stain, the smell, were still there for him, a place of bitterness for all its lush greenness, the fertility of those fields that had been bought in lives — in butchery. Land was maybe the final thing a man would lay down his life for, Odder thought, more even than his religion or his family — because, Odder supposed, it endured.

Then he hit the mountains, the real mountains. The first day wasn't bad, not too much snow. At the beginning, going in, he was contemptuous, remembering all the stories he'd heard about how wild the country was. Hell, he'd been through a lot worse in the West. Then he got in, really in, and his sense of superiority disappeared. He knew what all of them had been trying to tell him: this was the kind of wilderness that set itself against a man, a vast, dark world where the trees shut out the sun and the lakes lay like great smooth sucked stones, and the snow was five feet deep in places even though it was the end of May.

The forest was a wall of trees, most of them over a hundred and fifty feet high, with huge trunks ten, twelve, fifteen feet around, so high that Odder, looking up, could not see their tops. The sun was shut from sight. He went mile after mile dwarfed by those monolithic trunks, making his way over thick fallen hemlock and pine, fighting for a path through thickets that choked back any other growth save the massive forest of trees, the whole earth twisted with vines intertangled like writhing snakes, a wild dark place of roots and the rubbish of trees. Evil.

He got lost he didn't know how many times, and he was winded all the time, big and strong and tough as he was. It took courage just to keep going — hacking away, inch by inch through creepers, vines, shrubs, bush, bracken, thick spongy cushions of moss, swamps stinking of fetid water and rotting leaves with broken, black tree stumps sticking up in the air.

He felt the enmity all around him. Up and down, hacking his way bit by bit: he never seemed to get anywhere and yet he kept going. Sooner or later, he kept telling himself, he was bound to come out somewhere where there were people.

Nights he would stop and sink down in a stupor, hunch in, every muscle stiffening, his body a senseless quiver of aches, his head dizzy with the
day he had put in and the dark night closing around him with its furry
night sounds and its feeling that the trees had eyes to look down and laugh
at him.

After a time he would rouse himself to take out the flint and start a fire;
sometimes he just rolled himself in his blanket and slept, not even bother-
ing to chew on anything before he fell into an exhausted sleep, lying under
those almighty menacing pines, sunk in an unconsciousness through which,
in flashes, the pain of his body nudged him and he rolled over with a groan
and felt the whole dead weight of the forest and his fatigure bearing down
on him.

Dawn in these woods didn't come the way it did anywhere else. In open
land light came with a jolt and a stab; in forests, most forests, it dripped in
slowly, probing at the undercover world uncertainly; here the darkness grew
gray, but there was never really light. Some places Odder doubted had *ever*
been touched by the sun in so long that it no longer mattered. The woods
crowded together to keep out light, moved its branches this way and that to
prevent the sun from getting through. But at least with dawn the sense of
foreboding lifted a little, not much; enough, however, to shift shadows, the
great bulk of the wood rousing themselves to press up to what they needed
for still more growth, the unseen sun.

Odder would shift and press his eyes closed, trying to shut out the
knowledge that it was time to get up, eat (if he could get his stomach to accept something), press on. He lay cold, aching, unable to make his will
work, until a massive assault of pain made it easier to shift and rise than lie
still. He stood, blinking, under the great trees, hating.

He had forgotten how strong an emotion hate was, hadn't really felt
this intensely about anything since the year he'd left home. Love he knew, a
little, leastwise, he told himself. But hate was something strong and sure,
something he didn't mistake. It could keep a man going day after day, he
was learning, without any hope at all (hope was what love was, wasn't it,
leastwise the way he understood it). Maybe there was an element of hope in
hate, too, because a man knew he was going to get his own back on the
thing that was eating away at him. Like these woods. Because there was one
growing certainty in Odder and it was this: he wasn't going to go through an
ordeal like this without paying something back, and if the woods put him
through it, then it was the woods he would pay back.

A man with an axe could see to that.

He had been moving five, maybe six miles a day (time had become a
strange insubstance under these trees, a dream he could only partially keep
track of) when he came out on top of one of the endless mountains he had
been moving up, down, up, down, up again, and there was the lake below

him—long and slender and silver, like a great fish that dipped and disappeared into the tangle of trees, the darkness of ridges beyond.

The sight took his breath away. He didn't know what to do with beauty—he never had—it always made him feel a little ashamed, as if he had been given something he didn't deserve. He stood staring, looking at the great slash of silver in front of him, not even thinking, just looking, unable even to compose a phrase about it in his mind, just standing there breathless and moved. Then after a time he started down, thinking, There's where I'll have my place, not this side, *people* on this side, but over there, on the other side, where there's nothing, just this silver water and the farm in back cut out of that mountain, take down those trees and make me my farm there, looking right out on the water. There won't be any place you plow you won't be able to look out and see that silver water.

Odder went into the little cluster of loggers' and trappers' shacks, a place they called Algonquintown, though strictly speaking it was in old Iroquois territory. Some trapper from up north, not knowing or caring the difference in Indians, had named it. It wasn't much to dispute over anyway, just a clearing in the wilderness where men who scraped a living from the elements hung together. It didn't stay Algonquintown long anyway. After Odder started coming across the lake for supplies, the trappers, hunters, and halfbreeds stopped calling it Algonquintown and started referring to it as Odder's Landing. First it was Odder's Landing, then Odder Buttes's, then at last, permanently, Buttes Landing. Which was right: Odder was the only one in the area who took root; the rest were just sort of passing through.

He spent two weeks walking the east side of the lake, figuring out just where he wanted his farm. When he had the markers clear in his mind—Indian River, past the big rocks and the slide on one side and the long natural boundary of shale on the other—he figured he'd given himself more than enough to keep him busy for a lifetime.

He saw just the spot for his house, at the end of a cove, a natural little inlet where he'd be protected from the open lake but where he had the great expanse of water in front of him. A man looking out on that, he figured, would be all right.

Having worked it out in his mind, he set about getting it put down on paper, where it would all be legal. It took him two days to walk back to Burroughs' general store. The land was for sale all right, Burroughs said, spitting, if anyone was fool enough to want it. It's no more than rock and scrub, what you seen for yourself from the look of you, and then big unbudgeable trees. You figurin' on buyin' *that?*

Burroughs was a spiderlike rusty-looking man with red hair and close-set eyes; now in those squinting eyes there was a thin red little speculative flame.

I'm figurin' on buyin' if it's the right price, Odder said. He waited a moment before he set himself up as a real fool. To farm, he said, setting the words between his teeth.

That ain't plantin' land.

I'm aimin' to farm.

Go down valley—

You know who owns that land or not?

I own it, Burroughs said, I'm the land agent man here leastwise.

You got the papers?

I got the papers.

Then how come you're runnin' down your own land?

Burroughs laughed. Now if a man's got money—

I got money.

He shrugged. A speculator, heh? he said.

No, I told you, I'm fixin' to farm.

Burroughs shrugged again. It's beyond me, he said.

I 'spect so, Odder said. You want to talk price or not?

Talk never hurt no one.

You spent too long in the woods if you believe that, Odder said, and they went in to look at the township charts.

People came from miles around to see what the damned fool was up to, even though the trip back and forth took, by boat, the better part of a day. Burroughs came with a jug, told him (again) he was crazy, he didn't know winters up here, he didn't know the lake. Move back, he said when he saw the patch at the end of Blue Cove that Odder was clearing, that's no place to put a house. The lake'll git it.

The valley farmers came, shook their heads. You don't know nuthin' 'bout this lake or this land. You can't put your house there. You put your house there, the lake'll get it. Go back down to the valley, they said, that's where you farm. This here is woods land—

Odder worked on, clearing the patch where he would put his house, worked harder now, angered, the heavy heat all about him, the lake perspiring, midges and mosquitoes graying the air. July came upon him unexpected; with all the traveling, he had lost track of time. It seemed to him he ought to be rounding into June and here it was midsummer. He had a lot of work to do before winter; he began to get up earlier and earlier, push himself harder and harder. He wanted his site cleared by mid-autumn, stumps and all (he had decided not to waste time waiting for a winter to rot them out), and that was going to take some doing.

He pushed himself, eating in snatches, never stopping for a proper meal, finding that eating oftener in smaller amounts gave him more energy. In the morning and at night he set a small fire and boiled up tea. He had no sorghum or hard maple sugar to break off, which would have given him the pleasure of something sweet, but he drank the boiled tea as hot as his mouth could stand it and it kept him going knowing that there was the fire and the hot tea waiting for him twice a day, something of civilization and the outside world, a little symbol of the things other people took for granted. He found the hotter it was the more he appreciated it.

During the day he wrestled with trees—axing, sawing, dragging, piling, pulling. An ox or a horse was going to be essential when he got to the work up in the big woods but here, near shore, a man could clear by himself. The onlookers when they came were full of advice, but Odder soon found you couldn't count on them for much work.

What you want to come up here for, a hard place like this, on this side of the lake, away from everyone? they asked, looking at the gaunt, grim mountains, the thick forest running down nearly to the water. You can't farm *this*, they said. How come you come up here?

All they had to do was look around, but what could *they* see, a parcel of damn valley-lovers? Flat land, soft land, he thought contemptuously, that's all they want. Let them have it. How could you explain anything at all about mountains to people who hunched down and were content to live in the midst of mud flats when they had hills all around them where they could climb up and look out?

The valley people were afraid of the lake. The bones of a lot of men lay at the bottom of that water—men who had fought grim brutal wars to determine who would hold this land, the French and Indians, the British, Ethan Allen's boys, Roger's Rangers.

The farmers were afraid of the dead; they were more afraid of the floods. They had been told that in some storms the lake would rise over its rim, creeping up until only the hills held it in. All nonsense of course, as any one of them could have verified during one of those storms just by climbing to the top of the hill to look. It was easier, safer, to stay in the valleys and live by valley-knowledge.

Where he came from, back in Ohio, though you could walk for miles, you'd feel nothing but the imprisonment of the place; it was sun and sky that fell in on you and held you down, pinned against that flat earth. Odder's father had had a fine big farm back there in Ohio, and Odder didn't care whether or not he ever saw his father or the farm again.

Years of wandering on the road, keeping close to himself, giving little, getting little, expecting nothing. Use people, yes, and let them use you a little when it suits you, when you get something out of it, but don't never give.

It was a philosophy that took him through barren, lonely times without scarring him. A man who is not willing to give much to life can't blame it if it withholds a good deal from him. A bargain, that's the way Odder thought, a bargain I make; not to want to feel much. I done my feelin' back there in Ohio with *him* (*him* for Odder always meant his father), now I'm finished with feeling. I just want to be left alone. Not get involved. You don't get involved, you don't extend yourself, you got nuthin' to fear, a philosophy that had worked out well, all things considered. And might have gone in interminably working out well except—

—Except he needed a horse to get the logs down off his hills. He had selected, after days of scouting the woods, the biggest, best trees for logging off; he had logged the first of these himself up at the north part of the property after first clearing out a path down to the lake from the underbrush, the smaller growth and trees, the rocks and bad inclines, so that after his trees were cut he could get a driver in to bring them down. He figured on working as long as he had to, even into winter; he could put water on the path to make a smooth frozen slipway. He rose with the first light (often sleeping right out in the woods to save time) and methodically worked his way through the road; then he began axing at the thick trunks of the trees he had selected, working hard, losing count of time, July swallowed up before he knew it, determined to get the north grove out before the really bad summer sweating days, the dogs days, set in.

When he had felled all the trees he needed, he went out and contracted to have them slipped down; but when the logger came with his big oxen and began to take out the lumber, Odder was enraged at the haphazard way he worked, his slowness, the oxen's awkwardness and limitations. Finally he drove the man off. There was no other way to describe it; his face was red with rage, he was shaking his fist and shouting, trembling with fury—like my father, just like my father, he thought, shaken. It's in the blood.

I got to do something, he thought, I can't let something get through to me like this. It's because I'm pushing so hard, he thought. No one else will work that hard, and it makes me tighten up to see them takin' their time. I have to think of a way to get them logs out myself.

A good logging horse was hard to come by, but he would have to have a horse. He could see that.

Oxen were of course the common way to clear the land down in the valley. Those sluggish bovines were just the sort of animals people who lived in the hollowed-out parts of the earth would own. But oxen were useless on land such as his. He needed the intelligence and mobility of a horse. Absurd, everyone said. Burroughs over at the Landing of course thought he was crazier than ever. "Take a horse over there?" he asked, incredulous. Then, "Where you gonna git one?"

It was a good question. No one except the rich and an odd crank here and there had a horse, let alone a logging one. Horses cost a lot of money and they couldn't take the punishment oxen could; they injured themselves easily, needed more care than steers, were likely to die of unexpected ailments and leave a man in the lurch. But the very precariousness of having one was in some ways what appealed to Odder. He asked around and all he heard was that the mill man, Guy Guthrie, had a horse, but he wouldn't *never* let it out. Anyway, you don't want *that* horse, everyone said. There might be some down near to the Falls, it was finally conceded, so he went there.

He wanted an animal that had training, one he could depend on, one that would keep on the slipway, that was capable of maneuvering the bad places and of learning the route and following it, then forgetting that one and learning a new one. Logging horses had to be big and powerful, reliable and, above all, calm.

His was a fool's errand. He lost valuable time looking, and he fretted and raged around the countryside, stamping up and down the valley searching, aware that in his stubbornness and anger he was just like *him*, unable, even as he recognized the similarity and absurdity of his behavior, of changing it—maybe families were doomed to repeat generation after generation the badnesses in their blood because if you knew you were acting atrociously, why couldn't you stop? He knew all right, but he went right on ranting and raging. Like father, like son: the idea made him even madder.

Well, he didn't care. He *would* git himself a horse. But where? Where?

Those who had good horses of course didn't want to sell. He saw worn-out animals for sale, animals disabled by accidents whose owners still insisted they were sound; he saw horses with the heaves, blind in an eye or lame in a leg, horses whose smooth mouths showed their advanced ages, upper jaws protruding grotesquely, and yet their owners hopefully brought them out for barter, "they were jest a little gimpy or jest gettin' on a little or jest a little off their feed"; he saw animals mistreated to the point where they shied when a man came near and others that had so little discipline they reared and plunged when a man went to examine their teeth. He saw animals undernourished and overworked, ones with sway backs, splints, spavins, their wind given out, their forelegs gone or their spirits broken; he was taken to view animals whose owners advised him any child could ride them but whose nicknames in private must have been Killer or Outlaw; he came across one liar and swindler after another trying to masquerade as a kindly old horse trader, men who claimed they were only in the game because they couldn't stay away from a horse, but whose real larcenous hearts thrived on cheating, misrepresentation, deception, defrauding, plain old hoodwinking.

Yet he kept on. He did not let himself worry about how to pay for a horse once he found it. Nor did he let himself worry about how impractical a one-man operation would be, with no one to help. He would cut, load, go down and unload, and still save time. If you wanted something done, do it yourself; then it was done the way you wanted or if it wasn't, you had no one to blame but yourself.

So Odder Buttes plunged on from one farm to the next, doggedly determined to find a horse, resolutely setting aside the constant nagging notion he could no more do it all on his own than he could do anything worthwhile. Like having a son: which brought up the question of a wife. He would have to have a wife to have a son, and to have a wife he would have to have a house and to have a house he would have to have a horse . . . so in the end in order to have anything he wanted, he had to have a horse, and it just didn't stand to reason with the money he had that he would get that horse. So. . . .

So he went to see Burroughs again. Burroughs did him the favor of keeping his satisfaction to himself and of assuming an interested, worried expression, as if he gave a damn whether or not Odder got his horse or his house. "Well," he said at last, "Guthrie won't sell no ways, but you might try borrowin'."

Odder shook his head.

"You got somethin' else to turn to?"

Odder shook his head again.

"Then what you got to lose? Guthrie's an odd one, he jest might. Mind the bull though. Don't go cuttin' across his place, you never know where that damn bull may be."

Guthrie ran a small mill and was thought odd. For one thing, he had "family," a daughter—his woman had died years before. But even one member of a family made it family; there were few men for hundreds of miles around who could claim that. The daughter had a reputation for being wild and Guthrie for running young men off before they even got near his filly. Emily, she was called, the redoubtable Emily.

There is always for every man a woman somewhere he hadn't counted on, one who will look him over (much as she would look over a horse) and size him up and set her sights on remaking him and that was as good as the end of him. A woman with an image inside her head was a powerful force to reckon against; she could outwit, outwait, and outflank any man who tried to harden his heart against her—that is, if she was halfway good looking, well enough built, and overwhelmingly single-minded. Also Emily Guthrie had one thing working for her most of the women Odder had known didn't. She knew more, it turned out, about what he was trying to do than he did. That was a hard thing for a man like Odder to hold out against. She would be a help—God preserve him, a help . . . and. And so . . .

The horse and the woman were both, he saw in an instant, prime stock, and by any conceivable stretch of the imagination he couldn't afford either.

Anyway the moment he and Guthrie went out to see the horse, things got off to the wrong start. Guthrie certainly didn't want to sell the horse—he made that plain enough from the first—but he was so damned proud of his horse, he couldn't resist bragging about it, urging Odder to see it. Showing off, Odder thought disgustedly. These horse people are all alike, got no sense whatsoever. One man buys a blind horse and makes excuses for it, another rides around on a lame old nag and tries to say it's only a passing stiffness, and the next babbles on about his animal as if it were some kind of blamed miracle. To hell with him. He don't want to sell nor loan, that's his business.

Odder started down the road, the miller walking along bragging about what his horse could do, mares were sent from all around for servicing, wasn't a horse anywhere in the whole state could touch him. Odder stopped and said to him, "Maybe so, but kin he log?"

"Kin he log? Course he kin log. Ain't nuthin' any horse kin do, this horse can't do better."

The damned fool deserved to have his bluff called. "Kin he go on command, jest your talkin' to him?"

"Course he kin. Any halfway decent horse can do that."

Odder trotted alongside Guthrie, the pleasure of seeing this vainglorious son-of-a-bitch taken down a peg or two already filling him up. Jest like his Pa again, like to see men put down a peg or two. Ain't nuthin' his Pa liked more than see another man made a fool of, especially if that other man was his own son.

A heavy sun was hanging over the hills; not a breath of air was moving from field to field. Odder walked happily, chewing silently, remorselessly on the cud of Guthrie's coming comeuppance.

A man got what was comin' to him. Might have to wait a spell, but the wheel turned. Nothing had been said of the girl. At the last moment she just materialized. From where, Odder never knew. One minute she hadn't been there, just Guthrie and he walking under that merciless baking sun; the next she was standing by the barn, a tall scornful thing with thick black hair and big black knowing eyes. She had on men's clothes, rough men's clothes; they were hauled across her like they had shrunk on her, so tight you would have to cut them off, Odder figured, to get her out of them with the skin unscraped. Her thick black hair was tumbled up on her head and anchored there with a big bone pin. She had on gloves and she aimed, Odder saw, to his and Guthrie's surprise, to put the horse through its paces herself.

"I seen you come up the road," she said to Odder (which, to a more thinking man, would have been warning enough). "I know what you come about," she went on without waiting for a reply. "You're the man's been all over asking about horses." She said horses hor-says, as if he didn't know a damn thing about hor-says, and all up and down the county they had been laughing their fool heads off at his backassed ignorance. "There are hor-says and hor-says," Emily Guthrie said, hitching up her pants. "And I aim to show you what a real hor-se is like."

Then she was gone, vanished God knew where; in a moment she had materialized again in front of them, a big bay in back of her.

The stallion was enormous, seventeen hands at least—fourteen, fifteen hundred pounds—and had the look of the outlaw. How that girl had the nerve to turn her back on him was a question so frightening to contemplate. Odder immediately cast it out of his mind. If Guy Guthrie's girl wanted to let that creature kill her, it was up to her father to holler. Odder just wished he'd gone on his way and left the Guthries to kill themselves with their own conceit. It had suddenly come to him that that raw-boned stubbornness of theirs might end up crippling or killing him.

The bay was moving back and forth behind the girl, nervously shifting from one foot to the other, its wild eyes never still. When the stallion's flaming pupils weren't focused for a brief, feverish instant on one of them, they rolled back deliriously in a kind of spasm of power, as if the animal were anticipating the instant when he would rear and plunge forward on top of all of them.

Odder tensed, ready. He felt there would be a second of warning when those eyes finally stopped for the briefest instant and focused, just before the attack. Oblivious of Guthrie or the girl, his whole body concentrated on intercepting that warning. He did not think through what he would do. There was no need to: his body was already alerted, instinctively ready to direct action.

The girl was laughing. It took Odder a moment to realize that she was laughing at him. From the tone of the heavy, insulting sounds, he was sure her head was thrown back (he did not take his eyes off the horse); he felt a quiver go through him, a kind of reflex contempt of his own for his fear (but he still did not take his eyes off the horse).

Then she was touching him lightly on the arm.

There was no hope now and he knew it. He had to look at her. He couldn't call himself anything but *coward* if he didn't match her disdain of danger. In that instant he gave up—at the time he thought he was simply relinquishing any control he might have over the horse, but later he saw he had given up something he could never get back, the sense of being able to survive solitary, the pride of being sufficient to himself.

When she touched him on the hand and he felt he had to look at her, she had won the game right there from the start; but at that moment it was impossible to draw any such rational conclusion, to see any long-term implications, he was acting solely on the message of the moment. It was a long, long time before he began to understand and when he did, he was already glad of the changes she had made, he thought himself a better man for them, so that he rejoiced in that mastery and said to himself, When she touched me on the hand . . . meaning many things, not the least of which was, That was the beginning . . . and then—

He looked at her. Her hair had partially blown free; there were black wings in the wind at either side of her head. Her white teeth were large and glittering in laughter, her eyes big and bright—but she was laughing real laughter; it amazed him to find she was not laughing at him, but simply and naturally, *happily*, aglow with her pleasure in the moment. She was not making fun of him. There was a joke, yes, but it was not necessarily turned against him, but against all of them, all men.

"Watch," Guy Guthrie said with a chuckle, proud of his daughter for having played an old trick on a new man. (Later Odder learned how many other men in that valley at one time or another had been the victims of the Guthries' perverted sense of humor, heard with some kind of curious pride that he had stood his ground when most of them had turned tail and run.)

The girl stopped laughing. She was watching Odder calmly, scrutinizing him with her clear eyes of appraisal, and he looked back at her with the same quick sense of knowledge. It was as if they were saying with their eyes something their tongues would never be able to put into words. A strong, beautiful, frightening girl. And that laugh, *that laugh*—when you held her in your arms, he was sure, she would give that same sure laugh just before you put your mouth down on hers and stopped it—for a time. But you would never stop it forever.

Then he was ashamed. Guthrie was standing beside him and must have recognized what was in his eyes. When a man got that look on his face, other men usually understood. He turned for an instant to face out Guthrie and was caught instead by the quiet gentle stand of the horse. The big stallion was standing quiescently, enormous, but tranquil, a big, gentle, obedient beast that was amiable to any command.

There were all three silent, noting the change, a thing to be marveled at. Emily went up and put her hand to the horse's head, gently running her fingers over the muzzle; the stallion did not move. Its great stong legs seemed set in the earth, its eyes were still now but filled with what seemed to Odder a certain sadness.

Guthrie was speaking. ". . . always had a way with animals. Once there was this bull, out in that pasture there," Guthrie gave a vague, indicative nod of his head toward a small cleared sun-blistered field. "No man could come near him. You could take and tie him down so you'd swear he'd never get away and some man would go in that field and start walking toward him and that critter would catch sight of the man and commence rearing and pulling and throwing his head around and pretty soon he'd pull free, tear big chains right outen a log and scramble away, pulling the chain right after him, and he'd head straight for that man and never stop, no matter what he was pulling or dragging, just keep his eye on that man and keep coming and if that man didn't have the sense to turn tail and *run*, he was a goner.

"Nuthin' stopped him, nuthin', he'd keep on a man once he got him 'til he'd near kilt him. You could take and harass him with sticks and spikes and whips, and it didn't come to nuthin'; he didn't even take no notice of you, all he cared about was that man down on the ground, just keep at him and at him—"

Guthrie paused. "Emily, she pestered me and pestered me about that bull. 'Don't let no one go out there and *bother* him,' she kept saying to me, 'jest let him out so he can be free and nobody at him. It's chaining him and worrying him with sticks that way that riles him.' And finally I got so sick of her nagging, I said, 'All right, all right, I'll leave him free, but I'm not comin' in to get you if—'

"'I'm not goin' in,' she says quick as a wink. 'Jest let him out so he can get by the fence and leave him be.'

"So I let him out—if her mother were alive, I'd probably never have got myself in such a fix, women got more control over thing like that, but her Ma died gettin' her, and I raised her myself, this girl, right from the time she was a year old, had an Indian woman who helped me, but it ain't the same as blood, and this girl, she knows me inside and out, but the trouble is, I don't know her, women always have the upper hand in knowing things like that, seems. Somethin' born in them. Me and Emily been close, there bein' just the two of us left like that, but she knowed me better'n I knowed her, and she got the best of me on this bull the way she got the best of me on most everything.

"Every day she'd go down, two, three times a day, and stand there by the fence and talk to that bull, take him some corn. She never made him do nuthin' for the corn, she jest put it out to come and git, stood there talkin' to him while he et it. Day after day, week in and out, it begin to git on my nerves, that big brute gettin' bigger and bigger, I figured we'd never git him out of that field and into the barn come winter, so I says to her, 'Cut it out, don't give him no more, you're only makin' him worse, grainin' him up like that. All that corn's gonna mean the death of some man come fall.'

"'No,' she says, 'I'm goin' in and bring him out.'

"'You're what?' I says. '*You're* goin' in and bring him out?'

"'That's right, Pa. When the time comes, I'm goin' in and bring him out.'

"Well, that's when I put my foot down. 'Don't you go near that animal, *not one more time*, you hear? You go near that animal one more time, you take him any more corn, you don't come to *my* table and eat, you understand?'

"She never answered me yes nor no," Guy Guthrie said. "And to tell the truth, I never looked too close to see whether she done what I asked or not. So long as I didn't see — so long as I didn't look too close, we didn't have to make no issue out of it.

"Well, that tenth of November come, the time we all take the livestock in, give the grass a little time to git a new start before the big snows set in, and there was the bull to git barned. We both knowed it and seeing as how, as I said, I didn't want to make it no test of wills, I sent her off for the day. Some errand, I forgit jest what now. It don't matter, we both knew. She *seems* to be gone and I tell the men who's come up to help, we got to go in and git the bull. There's not one of them will go in and I can't blame them. They figure the same as I do, the man who goes in there's dead, it's as clean cut as that. So finally I says, 'I'll go in and git him.' No one says nuthin'. They jest stand there and wait, wait for me to go and git kilt; then I guess they figure they can shoot the damn thing and be done with it for good.

"He's out in the middle of the field and he don't come near when he sees us, just stands there with them wicked eyes watchin'. Watchin' and waitin'. That's what they were doing, all of them, those men and that bull, watchin' and waitin'.

"I opened the gate and went in. I had this long pole with a big hook on the end. As soon as he got anywhere near me, I was goin' to give it to him good, and I started, slowlike, across the field. I figured if I could git up to near where he was and badger him with the pole I could run him up toward the men. They had ropes and we was goin' to lasso him and tie him down and drag him up to the barn. It was a darn fool plan but the best we could think of.

"I didn't have much faith, but it was either git him in the barn one way or the other or have him die on me out there when the real cold hit. A bull like that, it would stay out," Guthrie said matter-of-factly, acnowledging hardiness and tenacity when he saw it, "but if we got a real dip in the temperature, its parts — well, they git froze in the real bad weather and then there's nuthin' you can do but shoot it. So I had to git him in. I had a lot of money in him, mean as he was.

"He seen me comin'. Christ, I could see him watchin' my every move as I come acrosst the field slow as a man can go and still keep movin'. It was like walkin' to certain death, knowin' you're goin' to die, there's no way out of it, you gotta go, but not wantin' to, goin' slow and reluctant, but goin'. That's the way I went.

"And then all of a sudden he springs out and he's coming', he's comin' at a full run and *nuthin's* gonna stop him. I put out that big pole with this big hook on the end and he jest come straight on it, snapped it right in two, we had to let that hook work out of his neck, it was buried in there so deep we couldn't git it out, he had to let his system work it out; and the first thing

I knew I was on the ground and he was atop a me. I got marks on my chest to this day to prove it. And then he stops. He's jest standin' there, on top of me, all this slop from his mouth drippin' down on me, and I don't move a muscle, I'm lyin' there not movin', jest lookin' up. I tell you, I *never* git over that moment. And there's this voice sayin' real quietlike, 'Paul, come on, Paul.' That was the damn fool name she give it—Paul—can you beat it, a critter like that with a good Christian name? This voice callin' over and over, real calm, 'Paul, you come over here, I'm over here, Paul, come on,' and after a moment he goes. He walked straight over, jest like he was in a trance and he goes, straight away from me, right across the field, and there's Emily standin' with a pail in her hand, and talkin' real quiet and calm to him, and he come up to her and starts eatin' from that pail she's got in her hands, and she says to me, quiet and calm, 'Go let loose of the gate,' and do you believe it, I got up and done it. I was so stunned, and then she leads that ragin' bull as quiet as a lamb right out the gate—the men all jumps back over the fence—and she goes down the road and into the barn and puts him up. Ain't nobody else's ever touched him since and we got him still, down over there to the back field. You want to see?" Guy Guthrie asked, "Or you satisfied lookin' what she ken do with the horse?"

The next morning, early, Guthrie and the girl brought the horse, whose name was Arthur—all the Guthrie animals seemed to have names like that, Mary, Paul, Arthur, Felicity—and the three of them began working. At first Odder said he'd take the horse up into the woods and do the logging, and Guthrie and the girl could stay back where he wanted the house and unload.

"Won't be no use," Guthrie said in the same laconic way he had said a moment before (and left it at that), "No place to put a house, the lake'll git it."

Odder argued with him, just as he tried to argue about the house, and with the same results. Guthrie didn't argue back; he just stood his ground, repeating his original unshakable judgment. Finally he said, "Try and see. He won't work for nobody but her'n me." Guthrie seldom called the horse, as he had not called the bull, by name. They were simply "he."

Arthur was standing docilely beside the girl and Odder went up to him confidently and grasped the halter to turn him around. The instant his fingers grazed the leather, the animal plunged away from him, striking out. The next instant Odder lay on the ground, the breath out of him and a rib, he thought, cracked or broken. There was a terrible searing sensation in his side. The girl was bent over him, her face expressionless, even the eyes unmoving. She seemed to Odder some kind of witch, the animal standing patiently behind her, looking over her shoulder at him, gently, reprovingly. If she asked him if he was hurt, he would kill her. No matter what the horse did to protect her. But she had sense, for once, to stay still.

He struggled, panting, to his feet. There was a hot stinging all up and down his side and he had a moment of blackness when he put his weight down on his legs and stood, a moment where he began cursing inwardly at the knowledge that he was sure to pass out; but miraculously he remained on his feet, gasping for air, his side burning so badly that he couldn't speak. Guthrie had turned his back and seemed to be gazing out on the lake in contemplation of the early morning beauty. The girl said nothing; she took hold of the horse and started leading him up the small trail. "You comin', Pa?" she asked over her shoulder and plunged into the thick foliage, the horse at her side.

"How far up you want us to go?" Guthrie asked, his back still to Odder.

It took Odder several seconds to get enough breath to answer. Finally, he said, between gasps. "Almost—to the—top. You'll see."

Guthrie turned and went past him without a glance. At the edge of the brush, he said over his shoulder, "I know jest how you feel. She done it on me with the bull." Then he was gone. He stayed up there all day, sending Emily and Arthur down with load after load. They didn't even stop for lunch. Emily gave him some thick bread spread with lard and an apple somewhere around the middle of the day. They ate while they were unloading. In the middle of the afternoon, she gave him some maple sugar, "to keep you going," she said. He was tired and hot, his rib hurt and he was stung, the flies were terrible. There were red welts on her face, her neck and the back of her hands, the rest of her covered by the tight rough men's clothes and so (he hoped) protected; and she was working just as hard, maybe harder, than he. When he tried to remonstrate with her to stop and take a rest, she only gave him one of her black-eyed looks and went on working. It was beyond him. No price had been agreed on—"We'll git what's right out of it, we're not worried," Guthrie had said, and refused to discuss the matter after that. Odder couldn't figure out what drove them. They didn't seem to be looking after themselves at all. All his life he had been protecting his own interests and watching other people jealously guard theirs; but these people seemed to be worrying about *his* interests. It didn't make sense. Why should they drive themselves for *his* house? (He thought of his bull-headed, hard-hearted father saying, It takes most men a lifetime to get a good-sized farm going . . . I got mine in ten years. And I built me *this* house and I made me *this* farm. And this is the biggest house in the valley, and the best built, and the best land . . .) But what did they want?

He paused. My God, what a pain there was in his side. He heard the grumbles of an empty, protesting stomach, felt the nerves in his shoulder, that shoulder that had never been right since the summer he was fourteen and had had it out with his Pa, and the muscles in his arms, strained to the point where he had little control over his hands, his badly swollen, bitten mouth so sore and dry that he could hardly speak. Still he made himself keep going when he knew he couldn't go on another moment. But what kept them at this terrible punishing pace? It was his land, his logs, his house. Why should *they* care?

He had lost all track of time. The horse and the girl would come down with the logs, he and the girl would unload, not speaking, she and the horse would go back up, he would start squaring the timber. He was a little unsure of himself as he began to chip away at the logs to make them square. He had cut the timber, as he ought, on a waning moon, but the best building timber should be cut in February on the "old moon," and he had not been willing to wait six or seven more months to fell his logs. He had deliberately cut at the wrong time, and that made him wonder how good the wood was going to be. Fence rails would have been all right to cut during the second running of the sap in August, but good building wood you weren't supposed to cut in the hot months. Still, as he examined them, the logs seemed all right. He rolled them up onto the two big logs lying perpendicular, with spikes stuck in both logs to hold them so that they wouldn't roll while he worked. He found the rolling and lifting hard work, probably as hard as anything he'd done in a long time; but he liked working the sharp shot-handled wide-bladed broad axe and he was fairly proficient with it. He could square all four sides of the good-sized log in a little over two hours. It wasn't hard work, but after a time it became monotonous; all he did was make a series of back-cuts along the grain, split out the chips, and make a new series of cuts until the side of the log he was working on was finished off the way he wanted it. Then he turned the log, started in on the second side, finished that, and went on to the third and fourth. The only variation in the process was the last cutting; here the chips were hewn away with the edge to give a better finish although the marks of his work were still plainly visible. To give logs a smoother finish, an adze was needed, but an adze was tricky business and only employed on beams that were to show. Since Odder planned to plaster his house, he did not trouble with the adze.

After a time, immersed in work, he would suddenly be conscious of an intruding sound over the endless short chopping sound of his broad axe; he would look up and there would be the horse dragging new logs out into the clearing and a moment later the girl behind him.

Odder had no idea how many times this happened when suddenly his arms gave way on him, his fingers opened of their own accord, the axe slipped from between them and fell to the ground. For a moment he stood in the midst of that humming, crying wilderness—insects and birds, small animals shrieking, buzzing all about his head—and then he dropped to the ground, bent over on his knees, his side swallowing him up in one great grinding clutch of pain. He fell forward and wept. She had beat him again. And on his own terms this time.

The second day she stayed down at the clearing with him. "Arthur ken find his own way now," she said stiffly before the protest came out of his mouth. And she gave him one of her looks. There was no way to fight her. He watched Guthrie and the horse go off into the woods; then he picked up his axe and went over toward the pile of logs. She stood quite still, very straight. He was thinking she would probably come and take the axe away from him and do twice the job he could, and he was seared by a shame worse than the pain in his side, a murderous kind of helplessness he could do nothing about.

"That side, I want to see it."

He stopped and turned, staring at her.

"That side, *I want to see it*," she repeated and he could hear her saying a long time ago, Jest let the bull out so he ken git free and leave him be, and Odder knew why her father hadn't argued with her or tried to discipline her and why when she said something, people listened to her very careful and did as she directed, even though one of those had been her father who ought, long ago, to have beat that willfulness out of her. Women like her shouldn't be allowed around. A man was just no match for them once they had found out what it was like to get their own way. It was all her father's fault, he had let her have the chance to tame the bull, and she *had* tamed it and now she knew. Odder just shook his head stubbornly. Words wouldn't be any good against her.

She stepped forward and said so quietly that he had to strain his ears to hear. "Please, I want to see your side. I just want to help."

For something so untameable, so wild, so damned perverse, and *always* right, she was a beautiful thing. He thought about what her strong fingers would feel like on his flesh. He closed his eyes and put temptation way.

She took another step forward and gazed at him. She was so tall that her black eyes were almost on a level with his. Buttes let himself do what had to be done. There was no use trying to fight back. He didn't want to anyway. He took her into his arms and listened as he brought his mouth down on hers. He was expecting laughter. But there was no sound save that of the summer moths and the swarms of cicadas in the trees, the incessant whine of flies and the scandal-mongering shrieks of the busy birds.

The third day Guthrie didn't come back. Buttes supposed that the girl in her inimitable way had let him know there was no need. The house was to be theirs and she didn't want outsiders involved, not even her own father.

When she came into the clearing she had the horse and his tackle, a sleeping sack of sorts fastened to his back and some pots and pans. She was carrying a bundle which later he saw contained flour and maple sugar, some honey and salt, a kind of coffee made from ground dandelion roots.

She had come to set up housekeeping and like a good wife she began nagging him right away. The lake was no place to put a house. They had lost most of the summer, but with two of them they could get something going farther back up in the woods where—

He cut her short. "The house is going to be here," he said. She could have her way in everything else, she could do with him what she wanted in every other thing, but on this he had made up his mind, the house was going to be here. He prepared himself for the worst struggle of his life. She could leave, she could take the horse with her, she could do anything she wanted, *but the house was going to be here*.

"You made up your mind, ain't you?"

He looked at her.

"All right," she said. "The house will go here. But the lake's goin' to get it."

They had worked so hard the last weeks of that hot insect-ridden summer and into the cooler, rainier days of September that they were too worn out to care about anything—eating, sleeping, even touching one another. At the end of one of those back-breaking days, they would lie down on their pallets and stare up at the rough roof of the darkening sky. He didn't know how he could get through another day. And in every task he set for himself, he found she set a harder one for herself, keeping up with him from dawn till dusk and still going on after he had finished. She was up before he was, fixing food; long after he quit, she bustled about getting them something to eat. When he was too tired to make an effort to chew, she cajoled him and comforted him, told him the beans were nearly done, he had to eat to keep up his strength. He wanted to finish, didn't he? So he ate. And watched, disbelieving, while she got up and tidied the fire, worked sand over the pans to scrape them out, then went to the spring and fetched water to wash up, and finally sat down, feeding the fire, dreaming a moment into the rose flames before she let down her long black hair and began to brush. Night after night he fell into a deep impenetrable sleep to the steady sound of the strokes of the brush going through her long black hair. An Indian woman had taught her that one inflexible rule of living: always brush your hair before you go to bed.

In the morning the fire was always going; that meant she must have been up in the night feeding it. Once or twice a week Guthrie came up in the late afternoon and brought them a slab of meat or part of a deer. He brought tea, too, real tea, and Emily would drop whatever she was doing and go to the fire to boil up water and fix them a pot of good hot strong tea. She had been very good at finding substitutes for real tea, which was far too expensive for them. She had little packets of birch bark, tanzy, camomile, and sassafras that she used. He liked these better than the dandelion drink or the coffee made from chickory root or ground locust seeds. She said they tasted almost the same as the real thing, but he was not convinced. They drank Guthrie's tea gratefully, sitting in the late afternoon light looking out over the lake. It was full fall and the first flights of Canadian geese flew overhead mornings, sometimes settled in on the far side of the lake at night. Odder heard them coming long before he saw the queer thick V-formations overhead. The birds migrating meant he and Emily had three, maybe four weeks left to work if the weather held, but he felt they were going to make it; and as they sat by the fire, with the mugs of hot tea steaming in their hands, they would take time out to talk a little, he and Emily, of what they —and Arthur—had done. For without the horse, without the girl, Odder realized he could never have come halfway near finishing. He tried to put in words what he felt, but it wasn't much use. He wasn't any good with words. In any case, it would have been impossible to describe his tumultuous feelings. All his life he had worked toward *not* feeling; now suddenly he was nothing but feeling. His bitterness against others, his belief that standing alone was the only way to remain safe, all his defenses were breaking down. He was unlearning many things, lessons from the merciless brutality and lovelessness of his childhood that had shaped his whole life. It seemed to him he had to be reborn, to be what he had never been before, another kind of man entirely so that he might equal her vision of him, to be even fractionally worthy of her. Impossible to *say* any of this—he would have to show her, and the horse—how grateful he was and do it the only way he knew, with his hands. He puzzled it over the long days working, thinking about how he had come to love a girl and a horse—a horse!—and that in some mysterious way they loved him back, too, even that ornery old animal whose first instinct, Odder was sure, was to stomp him to death. Now the horse came and laid his head against Odder's back, scratching, nearly knocking Odder over; but it wasn't meanness, it was affection. Affection in a horse. Crazy, crazy.

What could he make for them, or give them, to show how much he cared? He would have to find something special, but what? He wanted to give her something no other had — and Arthur, Christ, what could you give a horse to show you cared?

That in itself proved how far he'd come since the beginning of the summer, that he could even think like that. But sometimes it seemed to him he was too tired to know what was really happening to him. He got up, he worked, he ate, he slept, he worked in his dreams and arose tireder than before, and always he went back to work again. They had got all the timber they would need squared; they had cut the lumber that would be driven across the lake after the ice formed and left to season over at Guthrie's, to be cut into clapboards in the spring. Odder had figured at first he would cut the clapboards himself, but that was precise and tedious work because the boards had to be placed on the house in graduated widths to preserve the proper proportions, the upper boards narrower than the lower ones, and he wasn't sure he could do the job anyway. It seemed an insult not to give Guthrie the work, the girl working so hard putting up the house. So the clapboards would be mill cut. Still there was an enormous amount of work left. There were three mammoth piles of logs stacked on shore ready for the January freeze. He and Arthur would transport them across the ice on a log sled. He had dug most of the foundation of the cellar that would serve for winter storage of their root vegetables, but there was still the final work to be done, no real problem — the cellar floor they had decided to leave dirt, but Odder wanted the walls stoned in. The shore was lined with every conceivable size and shape of stone; it was just a question of gathering them, backbreaking work, yet some of the best days they had were when he and Emily and Arthur went along the shore collecting rocks.

The weather was warm during the day, but the nights were crisper now, and the bugs (thank God) gone; they were able to let up a little on themselves. He even remembered the first time he laughed. It struck him then how long it had been since he had been able to do that. The house was always with him, an obsession, she said, frowning, then brightening, smiling, as if, after all, obsessions were the rule, not the exception of life.

She was right; he was obsessed. Nothing else mattered, not even the girl herself sometimes. He had forgotten any other call on him, and then one day, down by the water, when she suddenly rebelled against something he wanted to do and stuck out her tongue, he laughed, and saw how out of proportion his life had become. He couldn't understand why the girl had stayed with him, lopsided as he was, a kind of fanatic, but then he didn't really understand Emily at all, he knew, any more than he understood any of the things that kept him going — his heart or lungs, even this senseless obsession — she was just part of him, of what made his life go on, he ac-

cepted her the way he accepted his lungs breathing for him, his heart pump-
ing his blood; but when he laughed, he also knew for the first time what
would happen to him if she ever took it into her head to leave him. It would
be the same as if he quit breathing; he stopped laughing, suddenly, afraid.

"You don't have to do it," he said. "None of it. I don't know why you
do it."

"Everything interestin's a challenge."

"You figure you're gonna tame me, have me eatin' out of your hand,
come to your callin', gentled, like that bull, like this here horse?"

No answer: she had turned her head, he saw only the blowing strands
of black hair. She was right to brush it that way, it was beautiful. He was still
filled with his fear, he wished she'd say something. Maybe he ought to try to
tell her what having her with him working that way had meant to him, but
he didn't have the words, he wasn't even sure there were words for that kind
of feeling in a man. Still he didn't like this small, humble, frightened feeling inside him; he had to do something to make it go away.

He just stood, a damn frightened fool. Finally he said, "You figured
yet on when we're supposed to—you know, make it *permanent*," he said
with difficulty.

When she turned her head, her eyes, big and black, looked right into
him, "I guess I figured *a man* should do that kind of decidin'."

The horse was getting agitated, he wasn't used to all that standing
around and talking.

"I never figured a man ought to ask a woman 'til he's got a house he can
take her to," he said stubbornly. "But then if you—"

"Then you done the decidin'." She went up to Arthur and began to
scratch his withers, moving her hand slowly and methodically toward the
root of his mane; Arthur laid off twitching his tail and moving his feet
about, quieted. The horse and girl stood there, watching him.

"But you got your rights, too."

"I know my rights well enough. You heard me complainin'?"

It was beyond Odder, he gave up. But he was suddenly tired and sat
down.

"Let's go in the water," she said.

"*What?*"

"Let's me and you go in the water. It looks nice and cool and it's so hot
and anyway we could do with a good wash."

Here he was talking about marrying and she wanted to go bathing. She
was already taking off her boots. "You gonna go on in now. I mean, jest as
you are?"

"How else do you want me to go?"

"But it's plain daylight and—"

"Nobody around, maybe an Indian or two, and it's nothing to them," she said matter-of-factly. "It's good and warm, no better time."

"Emily," he said, choked.

"I wondered when you was gonna notice."

"But how come you never said? How come you—"

"You had the house on your mind," she said, "I didn't want to worry you with nuthin' else. And I thought you'd find out for yourself soon enough. You don't hide nuthin' like this long."

There was no preacher in the area and if they were to go to the Falls, there was something about posting banns, take a long time and cost a lot of money—Guthrie and the girl decided to bring one of those circuit-riding fellows back and have the wedding over at the mill. Odder was a little upset because all this meant more delay on the house and because he had finally come to the only conclusion he could: he would have to put up a log house for the winter. He couldn't camp out in the cold with a wife and baby—no, there was nothing to do but put up something temporary for the winter. She and Guthrie would get a preacher while he stayed behind and worked. Before he'd seen how she was, he'd never really thought much about winter. He'd had the vague notion she'd go back with her father and he'd get some winter work and then in the spring they'd come back together and begin putting up the house. Now he had to make a considerable revision of plans.

He decided first off to get a place up for them and quick; they could let the beams stand down on the house site by the lake and season over the winter there. In the spring with all the wood dry, they could get the house up fast with a little help. The cellar was in, it was just a question of getting the boards for the frames ready and raised. But being a Buttes the unexpected upset him. He hadn't figured on having a wife and baby before he had a house, and with Emily nursing and a baby to look after, he couldn't expect much help out of her. Come March she'd hardly be up and around; the baby was due in February, the worst part of the winter, he thought with foreboding. If he'd planned it—well, he hadn't. That was that. The week before she went off with her father to arrange the marrying, she kept putting his hand on her abdomen. *Don't you feel him?* she'd ask, impatient. Odder felt nothing but the deep rhythmical give and take of her breath, but to make her feel better he said he did. He could tell he had done the right thing, lying; she was happier than he'd ever seen her those three days before she went off with Guthrie.

The first day she was gone Odder felt a strange sense of relief. She had made him very nervous putting his hand on her all the time that way and asking, *You feel him? He's kicking hard.* and his lying and saying, Yes, He sure was strong, wasn't he? He had begun to get jumpy, so he was glad to see her go, though he felt ungrateful and disloyal at his relief. He realized now how many months it had been since he'd had no one to answer to but himself. (They'd taken the horse, which was just as well, all things considered; Arthur liked him well enough with Emily around, but there was no counting on his reaction if she went off and left him alone with Odder.) The opportunity of not having to consider another human being (or animal) was a pleasure he could not deny. He felt suddenly, extraordinarily happy, as if some insoluble problem had been settled or some great grief lifted from him. When he arose that first morning, the woods were unfamiliar to him, as if he were seeing them for the first time; he marveled at them, glad to be in them all by himself, nothing to spoil his sense of satisfaction that first day, and everything went unaccountably well as he went about the first morning chores. Things that usually annoyed him, he paid no attention to; decisions he had put off suddenly and easily presented solutions almost by themselves; he felt none of the pressures and tensions he normally experienced on waking when it seemed to him there were more things to be done in the day ahead than he could accomplish. Instead of hurrying, hastening through breakfast, rushing himself into the day ahead, showing off, he supposed, before Emily, he took his time, nor did he feel guilty, recognizing only now that he had felt guilt about the way she was up before he was getting the fire going or the way, after he quit at night, there still seemed so much for her to do. He didn't worry about her at all. That was the best part, no one to worry about, just himself to pleasure.

He got up and built a small fire, made himself some strong birch tea, spooned honey into it, sat down on a log looking up the hill to "her tree," the big larch—the tammyrack, she called it. Perversely, or characteristically, she liked it because it was the only one of the pines that shed its needles. Why should she like that? It looked so bare while the other pines near it were still green and full. Still, he had to admit it did have a grace the others lacked, something to do, he thought, with the daintiness—if you could use that word about a tree—of its branches. He himself preferred the big maples. Their huge-fisted boles were like dissected hands from unknown giants.

He drank his tea, munched bits of hardened corn cake. Emily had made them for him before she left. Corn meal was the staple of their diet. She cooked the cakes before the open fire, the corn meal simply mixed with water, patted into cakes, and baked on a board before the live coals.

He dipped one of the hard crusty cakes into the birch tea to soften it, taking his time, relishing the clear early morning air, the busy morning noises of all the birds and animals while he himself luxuriated in silence, in idleness, in the sense of peacefully evading responsibility. Yet he was not unbusy; his mind if anything was overactive. Ideas, plans, schemes teemed in his brain as he sat sucking his tea through the lump of cornmeal cake he had anchored between his teeth.

He savored the full measure of his liberty, putting down his empty cup and deciding once and for all the kind of water they would have in the house, a decision he had been putting off for months. The lake water of course was readily available, but there were problems about getting it up to the house and in winter—

A well was a lot of work and not to be counted on even if you put off digging it until August, the driest month of the year. If you found water then, you were likely to have it all year around, but a real long dry spell—two , three years of drought—could run any well dry, and then where were you? Of course he had the lake water he could always fall back on, but a man didn't like to put in the work of digging a well and shoring it up if he wasn't sure it would hold water all the time. No, gravity feed was the only answer. Find a good spring up in the hills and run it downhill by trough to the cabin.

He would give part of this clear bright morning to finding a suitable water for their cabin. A spring, yes, that was the answer. He would put a giant hogshead in the kitchen, in the barn, with wooden drains for the over-flows; there would maybe be a breezeway out from the kitchen or a summer kitchen off the wellway. He would see what Emily wanted.

Sham summer. Beautiful, though in the old days he supposed the set-tlers didn't think so. Indians didn't like the cold, they wouldn't go on the warpath when the weather was bad; but when it warmed up briefly late in October, then they roused themselves for a last skirmish before winter thrust them back into their long houses for the long dark months. Warring parties were usually in a bad mood in October after being closed in with the first cold. They could be counted on to commit worse atrocities than usual. Prob-ably why this weather was called Indian summer, because the Indians were out and up to no good. He remembered coming across the Mohawk Valley, that sense of blood being ground up in the very earth.

Funny how Emily's attitude and his were so different on the question of Indians. He wanted no truck with them, but she had a whole part of life bound up with them because of that Indian woman Guthrie had got down from the reservation to help raise her. Come with a girl near her own age, Emily had said, the two of them had growed up like they was the same blood. It made Odder cringe to think of her feeling that way. In some way that he didn't like to admit, she was almost Indian herself. All those barks and roots and herbs that she used were secrets handed down by the Indians. Half the things she told him about the woods were Indian things. So much of her Indian-made. She loved the grouse but thought them too beautiful, for instance, to be wild, surely an Indian idea. To her wild things had to be tough and toughness meant ugliness. She could never understand how the partridge and deer had endured. She was afraid for them all the time. Her concern over animals, her way with them, something in her hands, only a few people had it. Mostly Indians. Not white people, though, not any he'd ever met, leastwise. Except Emily.

She was a whisperer, too, the way the Indians were, standing next to a horse making those strange windy Indian sounds into its ear, witching it. The animals understood. He wondered whether animals knew other things about her he didn't, if there were ways of expressing emotions less limited in animals than in man. A man's vocabulary for his feelings was so small.

A brilliant sun raked the water below; yet a deceptive softness lay over the landscape as if it were spring. The beauty of the weather, the sun shining on the leaves so that they seemed glazed with gold, shadows hanging in the pines, the whole atmosphere made him ache as he gazed now at the renewed green of the grass under his feet and at the small open knoll at the top of the hill the green leaves sprouting from a dead branch near his feet.

There came the insistent sound of moving wings, grouse—Emily's bird, he thought of it, just as the larch was Emily's tree. He saw the male first, fan-shaped tail, ruffed neck. It was gone, trailed by a pair of hens, before he could see whether or not the feet had begun to change. In winter the birds put on "snowshoes"—horny combs that made their toes grow in order to help them over the snow. *Mitchiu ess.* Emily said the Indians called them, the canoe builders, because the sound of the male drumming in spring sounded like an Indian building a birch-bark canoe.

Wherever she was at this moment he knew she was sorry to be parted from him, pressing to get the business about the wedding arranged so that she could get back without wasting any time, her energy concentrated on helping him get what *he* wanted. Emily was willing to sacrifice any pleasure the trip might give her if she felt she should be doing something for him, and the worst part was that she did this willingly, happily, without thought, none of it out of duty. She was unselfish and self-sacrificing, uncomplaining and more energetic than he; it was a woman's nature to submerge herself in a man, find her life through his, lots of men would have said, but they wouldn't have been talking about Emily.

She gave, it came to him, because she was completely without self-interest in getting any return on her investment of giving; she was absolutely, completely sure of herself. Nothing frightened her or made her feel insecure (look at the way she had handled that business about having a baby) because she had a total reliance on her own ability to manage her life. She relied on her courage and common sense, troubles would come, disaster, there would be deep deep times of despair, but she would get through them all because if for thousands of years others had, why shouldn't she?

He stood under Emily's larch recognizing for the first time how much of his view of the world in the last few months was altered because he saw it now in relation to her—*her* tree, *her* bird, in a way *her* house more than his.

Yet she would never have looked at these as hers. She would never have seen the world selfishly, as he did—another trait inherited no doubt from his father, his father who could never break out of the prison of himself, who, in direct contrast to Emily, could see the world in nobody's eyes but his own.

Closed inside himself he had been incapable of really living—like his father, niggardly of himself, a denier of life, contemptuous of others, jealously guarding his small ways, never extending himself, a spoiler, one whose touch made base the bright metals of existence. A tarnisher, Odder thought.

He did not deserve Emily, he was not nearly as decent and loyal and self-sacrificing as she, but by God he did love her, and he would make her a fine house even if for this winter—all right, she would have to do with a cabin this first year, but there would be something in that cabin, he determined, and every time she looked at it it would tell her how he felt. Something alive, he thought. She is so alive. Nothing dead, static, something warm and touchable, something that returns love, something that would be company in the long months ahead while she was waiting for the child.

A dog would be best, of course, but the only decent dogs around were hunting hounds, hard to come by and a good price on one if you could find it, and what with the money he'd paid for the land, more than he should have laid out, but the temptation had overcome him and he had bought more than he originally planned, money was more than scarce, it was just nonexistent. And in the spring they would need to put in seeds, they ought to get a cow, there were tools necessary, the house would have to have things they couldn't make—

Money, there it was, always intruding, spoiling everything. The meanest and most persistent worry was money. It never went away, it could ruin most of the good and decent things in life, even things that did not cost, like the magnificence of this day, his pleasure at the thought of a pet for Emily, even the whole concept of the life he and Emily had ahead.

Get the cabin finished, he thought, then figure me a way to make money. There's always trapping, he thought. The woods would provide. Deer, bear, beaver, raccoon, otter, marten, mink, fox, even wolves—meat and skins; grease for frying, for soap and light bait, barter, and covering for the beds. The air provided grouse, turkey, geese, pigeons, ducks; the lake and rivers were filled with fish—trout, eels, bass, mussels.

I should be able to get us enough skins this winter to—and he felt better, a man with a plan always felt he had the future under some kind of control.

He trudged the spiny ridge of the mountain, barely conscious now of the loveliness of the lake, the gathering of the morning below; yet it was impossible to ignore for long. From where he stood he looked all the way across the point, over which an early morning blue haze now hung, across the two large islands at the end of the cove, all the way over to Algonquintown and the settlement of shacks, Burroughs' store, that meant "civilization." Let others have it, all of it: hypocrisy, betrayal, lies, cheating, deceits, the whole corrupt corner staked out as theirs. This was his.

Salt, milled grain and tools, stock—*that* was also civilization, he reminded himself, and he would never be able, no matter how hard he tried to be self-sufficient, to do without those, and because he would have to deal with men to get these, he would be tainted. He knew from the long years of knocking about what money could do to a man's morality. He had had one good friend in all his life and that friend and he had been at each other's throats over five dollars. At the time Odder had told himself it was not the five dollars, but the principle involved; but the fact was it *was* the five dollars; otherwise he wouldn't have cared that his friend had taken it. It cost money just to breathe: all the accoutrements and supports you needed to be allowed just to arise and walk about were exhaustingly expensive. Needs never ended and needs meant money to satisfy them.

They would have to have a cow, for instance. He could hardly invent that. Or make it. Or wish it out of thin air. Couldn't trap it. Might steal it, but that begged the point. To be owner of a cow meant that he had to have a certain amount of money to purchase it, to keep it alive. It ate, it got sick, it needed halters, harnesses. Why did he have to have a cow? Well, on his own he could have got along perfectly well without one. But the point—the *very* point—was that he was no longer on his own; in the course of the way events in a man's life moved, he had been moved: he was about to become a family man. A family man had to extend himself. Emily would need milk. Hence, the cow. And he ought to think about sheep, for wool; pigs for the larder; oxen, for farming. His life began to grow complicated, and more expensive. Making money—the need for making money—piled up. He was getting "caughter" and "caughter." All because a girl had looked at him in a certain way and laughed. Instinct had, maybe, had the last laugh.

If he was going to farm, no way out of buying oxen anyway. They were easy keepers, they were easy to yoke for heavy work, and in an emergency (God knew, he foresaw enough of these to make a few practical plans), an ox made better eating than a horse. The hide could also be salvaged and used. Yet for all their practicality, they would never, to Odder's mind, come anywhere near being a pleasure the way a horse was. Oxen were like valley people, something fundamental missing in them, something admirable and exciting and unpredictable. A dimension a man couldn't quite put his hands on. Horses had *character*.

Just as the men who lived in the mountains were a different breed from those who squatted in the valley—perhaps there was something about the mountains that forced the men who lived with them to form stronger characters and superior strength. At least Odder chose to believe so. The effort required to deal with hostile land was herculean, but the broader outlook on the world which the mountains gave back more than compensated for the strength expended to subdue them. Odder even believed mountain water was purer, the food grown in its soil stronger, and a man was as much what he ate and drank as anything else.

The house, he told himself, has to wait, you know that, stop woolgathering and get to work on plans for the cabin.

He had been turning over various designs in his mind and, now, pausing briefly, scuffling the autumn-hardening earth with his foot, he let his mind drift toward a decision; he didn't make a decision, it just more or less came. He would model his cabin on those Swedish ones that had been built along the Delaware, the ones so popular later with the Germans in Pennsylvania and the Scotch-Irish pioneers on the frontier. He had always admired the cabins those people put up: rough though they were, they were extremely durable, far superior to the bark-roofed dugouts and wattle-and-daub buildings supported by crotchets so many settlers threw together, to say nothing of the primitive bark and woven-matting wigwams of the trappers and hunters. Emily certainly wasn't going to live in something thrown together, no matter how hard pressed they were.

Like his father again, wanting his buildings to be permanent, to say something about the kind of man he was.

Well, why not? With just an axe a man could erect a very substantial dwelling. The axe was more important than a gun, a hoe, a spade, or even that scythe that Odder had left behind and still thought of with pain. You didn't carry bulky scythes when you went alone on the road. He wondered if anyone back there in Ohio ever used it and, using it, paused and read *O Buttes, 1795*, and remembered for a moment who he was.

He had taken very little with him when he left his family, but he had carried an axe. An axe felled trees to clear land for planting; it could build a log house. With a good axe a man could go right into the midst of the wilderness and begin clearing and building. With that one single tool he could begin to master the environment around him. He could make traps and snares with which to catch game; he could cut down trees, he could construct a shelter; he could cut and clear fields; and he could, if he was careful, hold the bright blade in his palm and use his axe like a knife to whittle nice things to comfort himself with, for a man needed those "extras," things some people said you didn't need, but which you did, things that filled the imagination and gave the mind's eye something to feed on.

He would use an axe now to fit together the cabin—cut the logs the right size, fit them together in a uniform stack, the ends notched to interlock, and the logs slightly flattened so that they would fit together snugly. He would use hemlock bark for the roof. The axe would make a fence, too, to keep the cow close to home. Fences would keep his own animals in and wolves and bobcats out, would prevent the deer from coming into his garden to forage. Later when the land was cleared of stones, the stones would make property boundaries and eventually replace crude stumps pulled together for fences, but in the meantime, he could hold Arthur and the cow in with a big stump fence with railing in between.

He began the morning working hard, with purpose, and by the end of the fifth such Indian autumn morning, he had the chimney for his cabin up, the sides more than half raised. He imagined Emily opening the door to the cabin and stepping onto the clay floor, the smell of newly cut pine welcoming her. She would smile when she saw the deacon seat he was working on nights and hoped to have finished right along with the cabin. He hoped he could get a table made by that time, too. He wanted everything to be ready, to be right. He was just sorry that they had to make do with a clay floor, but there was no point in setting in logs or getting boards from Guthrie for just one season. He was dissatisfied, too, with the greased paper windows, but glass was out of the question. He would put a small borning room off the kitchen before hard winter hit to make up to her these primitive aspects of her life and if there was time—but time was getting awfully short, he realized.

He found himself now pausing, looking, listening, waiting for her. He was pretty sure she'd come by lake if she and Guthrie had found a preacher. It was much faster than trying to go around the lake overland on Arthur. So, if he saw a canoe headed toward Blue Point, that would mean the trip had been a success. Very few trappers and hunters pulled in on this side of the lake. And not this time of the year, they'd be up north already laying out camps and getting their traps ready. People had quit coming, too, to look at his fool scheme to put up a house at the edge of the lake and to lay out a farm. Heard about Emily, he supposed. News always travels fast, news like that anyway. You take a lone girl out in the wilderness and you let her find a man, that kind of thing travels like forest fire.

On the other hand, if he heard the sound of breaking brush in the woods, that would mean she'd come by horse and they were in trouble. He kept scanning the radiant ribbon of lake, but the only activity came from a couple of boats moving north early in the morning, trappers getting a late start.

Be good to hear, too, what was happening outside. He'd been so bound up in his work he'd forgotten the world outside. On second thought, maybe that was better. Only news that sifted through was usually bad news, the kind that unsettled a man because it had to do with things he couldn't control but which were apt to influence his way of living. Let the world stay away. He wanted to feel he could control his own life and when the news from outside came in, he was robbed of that illusion. So long as he and Emily were here by themselves, with an occasional visit from Guthrie, they got along all right. He wanted to hold onto that.

She had been gone little more than a week; yet the loneliness inside him was terrible, that first euphoric feeling of freedom had died out, to be replaced with a sense of loss and deprivation. The effort of boiling water, eating the hard cornmeal cakes, of lying down alone and looking up through the tall fringed pine treetops toward the dancing stars, stars making a sudden demand on him to understand the universe, the vast incomprehensible earth and sky, the firmaments around him, to understand himself, and Emily, her place in his life—it all seemed too complex. He was afraid of his smallness and lay alone on the hard earth and wished for his woman to press close to. In her warmth his fears and anxieties faded; it was an unmanning feeling to acknowledge how much he had become dependent upon her; his insignificance in the face of the multiplicity of the world around him intensified the knowledge that it was she in the end who upheld him, that only with her did he feel stronger than that vast world that he lay looking up at, stronger and superior—a little strutter under the stars, he thought amusedly, because a woman kept me warm and unafraid.

A man was so afraid to die and yet so often glad to shut the world out with sleep.

He wondered what kind of preacher she would get. He and Emily had never talked about religion. Too busy. He didn't even know what she was. Papist? Irish mostly were. He wasn't quite sure what he himself might have been called. The Butteses were never what you'd call a formal religious family. His father saw to it they did their duty (his father always saw to that, Odder thought) as far as the church was concerned, they went to the Sunday doings and picked up the Bible learning that was necessary; but about real religion, there was little concern in his father's house. About the only time Odder could remember hearing the name of God mentioned was in connection with an ornery cow being cussed out or an unruly boy whose behavior was held up to the Almighty as an example of ingratitude: deep thinking, Odder supposed, wasn't a Buttes attribute. Deep believing—he wondered about that. *How deep did thoughts go?* In the end maybe that was what counted, to see into yourself, then maybe you could see into others, understand a little the whole make-up of the world around you.

Sleep would never come this way, and he needed sleep if he was to work well. He was all twisted up. A moment before he had been saying that "seeing inside" was what a man ought to put in prime importance. Now he wanted to push down that seeing because it was becoming too troubling.

He sat up. The fire had died down, a few sparks glowed, orange in the darkness. He felt, looking at them, less alone, and he roused himself and went to the fire, stirring it up, adding twigs and some small branches. There were just too many demands made on a man, that was the sum of it. A man couldn't fix his attention on all of them at the same time and the ones he neglected made him feel uncomfortable.

He stood under the stars trying to understand, and not understanding, a man who could not decide what order of importance the demands inside himself had.

Emily had tamed two or three chipmunks. They would scamper from log to log, nervous and alert, full of high, querulous advice, while Emily prepared a meal. As soon as she sat down, they would run all over her, pestering her for something to eat. Emily always broke off bits of cornmeal and threw the crumbs out, laughed as they fought for their share, shoving crumbs into the pouches of their cheeks, squabbling, scrapping shamelessly. She would lean forward and cluck to them, her voice low-pitched in contrast to their high scolding, but remarkably like theirs in intonation and inflection. When Emily began to chuckle at them, they stopped whatever they were doing and sat up on their hind legs, their bright knowing eyes fixed on her. They came close to Odder, but they never let him touch them. Yet they ran all over Emily. She had broken up almost all her cornbread for them her last night. "They have to fatten," she said, "for when they go underground." She had smiled, but he could tell she would be sad when they went. They were companions for her. What puzzled him though was the way she talked to them. Why didn't she whisper, the way she did with Arthur?

He asked her about it. "Only to the big animals, the horses, the cows, the bull," she said. "Only big animals understand, Arthur understands, Paul understands, but these little ones, no, they can't understand."

It bothered him she could get so close to animals, tame them so easily, and he couldn't. But of course she never demanded anything of them, never seemed actually to make her wants a contest of will against theirs; what she entered into was some kind of reciprocal arrangement he did not even begin to understand, where no actual demands were made, but certain things were expected as a matter of course, were taken for granted. It never seemed to occur to her, for example, that Arthur might kick. She admitted the possibility, but the actuality was beyond her. "I know when he has his bad days," she said. "I know when you have yours, so why wouldn't I know when he has his? I stay out of his way on his bad days just the way I stay out of yours on yours."

He gave it up. Apparently she had made no distinction between the behavior of Arthur and himself, and perhaps there was none. But still— *still* . . .

It bothered him more and more that she should have this secret world of understanding with animals. He didn't exactly resent her knowledge, but he wasn't exactly happy about it either. If she had wanted to give him an animal, for instance, she would have simply tamed one, with no trouble at all. One of those "monkeys" of hers, probably; he understood why she called the 'coons that: he had begun to look forward nights to the dusk and the coming of the ring of eyes, the raccoons. They came every night, hoping for scraps, curious, wondering what went on. They had amused Emily. She called them "little monkeys," and told him the Indian word was *arathcone*, "he who scratches with his hands." An Algonquin word, she said, but all the Indians she had known used it.

He thought now that it was odd that she had never tried to tame one. Though she laughed at them, she remained fundamentally indifferent to their mischievousness—their getting into the food, for all the effort she took to secure the pipkins against them, the way they crept up and peered into the fire, then retreated, hissing and fell to fighting with one another, their tiny hands so like a man's with the apposable thumb that could dig and creep and sneak, showing an intelligence and cunning that fascinated Odder. Why shouldn't she have a raccoon with its quick, almost human hands, to go through the winter with? True, they hibernated as a general rule, but in the warmth of the cabin there would be no necessity, though the animal's activities would probably be slowed down—a Godsend, when Odder thought of it, imagining what troubles one could instigate—and by spring, when the blood was up again and the animal began to get rambunctious, out it could go.

That night Odder looked at the ring of eyes with new interest. A plan was forming in his head. He could now distinguish the two ages of the raccoons, the older, parent ones and their half-grown offspring. The older ones were bigger, more combative; they had acquired a craftiness that was not altogether admirable, as if time had taught them to be mean as well as mischievous. What he was looking for was a young animal, one that had been born the previous spring, but was still with its mother. A litter usually stayed under family protection almost a year, from the spring of their birth until the coming of the next litter the following spring.

He threw some acorns and broken bits of cornbread and the usual jostling, spitting, scuffling took place. While the older ones contended between themselves over these crumbs, Odder threw some more among the younger ones. He wanted them to get a taste—and an appetite—for what came from a man's hands. Emily had told him two things about raccoons that he was banking on working in his favor: they had long memories and they formed strong attachments.

He was surprised to see how large some of them were. Those would bear watching. If they took it into their heads, they could be formidable adversaries, and he needed no warning about what damage those talons might do or how fast; even with winter fat slowing them down, they could move with lightning speed.

He respected intelligence. And was familiar with the countless stories of the raccoon's reputation for using his teeth and hands to drag a dog to water and drown it by holding its head under.

Odder threw them some broken pieces of maple sugar and almost instantly was rewarded with excited cries of "churrr! churrr!"

He tossed the big animals a new helping of acorns, and as they scrapped and quarreled, the young ones moved closer to him, taking the places their parents had vacated. Odder took a step closer, cropped to a half kneel, and threw cornbread and crumbled maple sugar just in front of him. To keep the oldsters occupied, he threw them some more food; then he put a line of maple sugar bits directly in front of him. He wanted to see if he could tempt one or two to come close.

The young ones regarded him with greedy but guarded eyes. The bigger ones crouched low, warnings issuing from a deep growling in their throats, the fur of their bodies upped in danger so that they looked even larger than usual. There were eight or ten of these animals and Odder was suddenly struck by the notion that if they decided to rush him, he wouldn't have much of a chance; overpowered, he could be emptied of his food without delay.

His supply was almost gone now, and he was just as glad. He scattered the remainder to the young and retreated to his log and pipe. The job was going to be harder, he thought, than he had anticipated.

But the next day a new idea offered itself and that night he put some maple sugar bits in a pan near him and waited. The raccoons were there all right; it seemed to him they had sent word to their friends. They began their wait patiently, but soon he heard mutters and hisses. He was beginning to recognize what extensive sounds these animals had to show their feelings— screams, snarls, growls, purrs, hisses, grunts, and that odd churring sound used to keep a family in contact with one another.

He picked up his pan and rattled it, then sat, without moving, for what seemed to him an eternity. At last he saw a shadow come around the far side of the fire, approach, stop, pause, contemplate, retreat. Though he waited and waited, the animal did not come closer.

He threw no food out that night.

The next night he broke cornbread and maple sugar again into the pan, rattled it, put it down a little distance away from him, sat down on the log to wait. This time he did not have so long. The animal came directly to the box and with swift hands grabbed, then scurried back, eating; Odder could hear smacking sounds from behind the fire.

The following night Odder put the pan close to his foot. He had a long wait, but the raccoon came. He was being pressed from in back; several other animals had overcome their timidity and were approaching him.

The next night was the crucial one. Odder had constructed a large slatted cage, big enough, he thought, not to look like a trap. He carried this to the fire during daylight so that it would seem a part of the surroundings, and he put it down where he always sat. That night he put the pan in front of the cage, but not in it. His raccoon was uneasy, but he finally came and ate. This time when he finished, however, he stood on his back feet and looked Odder over. He was large for a youngster, with a look that said he would be one of the last to bed down for winter and that he would be making the woods aware of his existence right up to the very end. A fellow who knew his own mind and abided by it, independent, no matter what everyone else thought and said, sassy—Jefferson, Odder thought. "Thomas Jefferson," he said aloud.

The raccoon had a name now, he had become individualized. Before, Odder had only thought about raccoons in general; now that he had a specific one in mind, his feelings deepened. He was not just trapping a raccoon, he was catching Jefferson.

Jefferson seemed to have some stake in the affair, too. He came lumbering out of the woods just as the last light of day was fading. Odder called him by name—he hoped it *was* Jefferson—and went over to the pipkin and took out some hard cornbread, a wedge of the dark brown sugar. Jefferson was peering from behind the bole of an enormous pine near the fire taking everything in.

When Odder put the pan down in front of the cage, he kept one finger on the edge, but Jefferson wasn't troubled. He came running, gobbled up the cornbread and then gave Odder an irritated look. His expressive face seemed to be saying, "What you done with the sugar?"

That was inside Odder's other hand and he bent down and put it inside the cage. Jefferson looked at him. Right up until that look, Odder's plan had been perfectly clear. At the moment he got Jefferson inside the cage, he was going to clamp down the overhead shoot. Now he wasn't sure he could do it. There was something cowardly about catching an animal like that. He left the sugar but he did not shut the door. Instead he went and filled the pan with water, gathered some old boughs and came back, finding the raccoon sitting on top of his log, washing and grooming himself. He was crooning a little tune, licking and singing and cleaning. He looked up as Odder crossed the clearing and passed in front of the fire. Then he began pacing back and forth on top of the log, looking first at the ring of eyes in back of the fire, then at Odder bending down putting bedding and water, more food, inside the cage.

When Odder stood up, Jefferson was already going inside the cage. Giving himself only a moment to reflect on how unfair he was being, Odder brought the shoot down and locked Jefferson in. The namesake of the great democrat never even looked up: He was too bush sucking sweets.

She came by boat, Guthrie paddling. Odder was up on the hill when he spied a thin dark sliver on the water, identified it as a canoe and at the moment of identification knew it was *their* boat. He went down to the lake, took off his clothes and beat the dirt out of them as best he could with a stick, hoping they would look better; then he washed, the water so cold that he was gasping when he got out. He ran around to dry himself, put the clothes back on, and set out for the inlet where Guthrie would put in. Then it occurred to him they would probably want him to go back with him and he walked the few steps back to the campsite for his pipe. He looked at the raccoon in the cage and tried to decide what to do. He couldn't go off and leave him there, it wouldn't be safe; besides he didn't know how long they'd be gone and Jefferson would have to have food and water and company: even wild things needed sociability, companionship. Left alone too long an animal turned sullen, stubborn, mean.

Odder picked up the cage and carried it down to where the boat would dock. He had decided this was as good a time as any to give her her present, maybe the best since it would show her how glad he was to have her back. He sat on a rock and smoked, Jefferson in the cage putting out his small claw-like hands trying to clutch his pants. He supposed he looked a damn fool, sitting on a rock smoking, with a 'coon pestering the life out of him, but that, too, seemed the way things were destined to be. Part, he supposed, of the whole business of having a woman of your own was to look a damn fool in her eyes most of the time.

GRIEVING THE GARDEN OF EDEN

In the beginning was management
The Old Man, The Son, and some soul
called The Holy Ghost
with   natch   elaborate plans
for institutional integrity
Them up there and us here down below
on the assembly line
with   yes   a contract of sorts
but empty of actual arbitration
and no right to strike
so in the end any of the complaints
fell on empty air and Him
as the book says
"walking in the garden in the cool of the day"
reminding old Adam that the tree
like the executive washroom
was off limits
That first union activist
with a heart full of insubordination
she rose up in wrath didn't take no
serpent to put the notion in her head
any woman worth her salt would hold out
against Willmar and Stevens and the rest
took the only remedy open and said
I will too touch and so
they were driven out
by some scab with a sword
without any legal redress
and what I want to know
and a lot more like me
is this:
What kind of employer
makes an unconscionable covenant like that?

MY FATHER'S HANDS

My mother screamed
locked in the bathroom
so that she couldn't get out
the thud of fists
a steady rhyme
striking the bones of her face

He socked his second wife
down the stairs
the baby bled out of her
on the bottom step
while she lay still
balled up like a foetus

His third wife
flashed blackened eyes
puffed, split lips
and was borne away one night
in a blood red ambulance
her side stoved in

He beat the cars that broke down
snapped the golf club
that made the wrong swing
the dog cowered
when he came in a room
the cat ran away

His first wife divorced him
the second ran away
Number Three (*he* said)
took him for everything
she could get

His children
(my brother and I)
forgave him because
he was the only father
we were ever going to get

Except that sometimes
deep in the night
I lie awake and think
that if women judged
the prisoner in the dock

They would have said
my father's hands
ought to have been
lopped off.

Adirondack Works

Abel, Hilda. *The Guests of Summer*. New York: Bobbs-Merrill, 1951.

Atherton, Gertrude. *The Aristocrats*. New York: John Lane, 1901.

Brandreth, Paula (Paul). *Trails of Enchantment*. New York: G. H. Watt, 1930.

Comfort, Lucy Randall. *Love at Saratoga; or Married in Haste*. New York: George Munro, 1879.

Downes, Anne Miller. *No Parade for Mrs. Greenia*. Philadelphia: Lippincott, 1962.

Early, Eleanor. *Adirondack Tales*. Boston: Little Brown, 1939.

Ferber, Edna. *Saratoga Trunk*. Garden City, New York: Doubleday, Doran, and Co., 1941.

Findley, Francine. *From What Dark Roots*. New York: Harper and Bros., 1940.

Fisher, Ella Warner. *Idylls from Champlain*. Boston: LeRoy Phillips, 1918.

Goodfellow, Dorothy W. *Growing Up Wild*. Pacific Grove, California: Boxwood Press, 1977.

Heald, Aya. *Shadows Under Whiteface*. New York: Vantage Press, 1956.

Hines, Dorothy Palmer. *No Wind of Healing*. Garden City, New Jersey: Doubleday and Co., 1946.

Holley, Marietta. *Samantha at Saratoga or Flirtin' with Fashion*. Philadelphia: Hubbard Bros., 1887.

Hyde, Floy S. *Water Over the Dam at Mountain View in the Adirondacks*. 1970.
——. *Adirondack Forests, Fields, and Mines*. Lakemont, New York: North Country Books.

Keller, Jane Eblen. *Adirondack Wilderness: A Story of Man and Nature*. Syracuse, New York: Syracuse University Press, 1980.

Lothrop, Harriet Mulford (Margaret Sidney). *An Adirondack Cabin*. Boston: Lothrop, 1980.

Ludlum, Jean Kate. *At Brown's: An Adirondack Story*. New York: Hunt and Eaton, 1890.

Mooney, Elizabeth. *In the Shadow of the White Plaque.* New York: Thomas Y. Crowell, 1979.

Oates, Joyce Carol. *Bellefleur.* New York: E. P. Dutton, 1980.

Rockwood, Caroline Washburn. *An Adirondack Romance.* New York: New Amsterdam Book Co., 1897.

———. *A Masque of Honor: A Saratoga Romance.* New York: Funk and Wagnalls, 1889.

Rich, Helen Hinsdale. *A Dream of the Adirondacks and Other Poems.* New York: G. P. Putnam, 1884.

Schuyler, Doris E. *The Adirondack Princess.* Brookfield, New York: Worden Press, 1982.

Smith, Isabel. *Wish I Might.* New York: Harper and Bros., 1955.

Snyder, Maude Alexander. *Near To Nature in the North Country.* Watertown, New York: Parker Press, 1928.

Teall, Edna West. *Adirondack Tales: A Girl Grows Up in the Adirondacks in the 1880s,* Willsboro, New York: Adirondack Life, 1970.

Tippetts, Katherine (Bell). *Prince Arengzeba, A Romance of Lake George* and *Beautiful Lake George.* Glens Falls, New York: W. H. Tippetts, 1892.

Tyler, Helen Escha. . . . *in them thar hills: Folk Tales of the Adirondacks.* Saranac Lake, New York: Currier Press, 1969.

———. *Log Cabin Days.* Saranac Lake, New York: Currier Press, 1969.

Trombly, Della. *The Hermit of the Adirondacks.* Boston: Sherman, French and Co., 1915.

Notes

Introduction

1. Roderick Nash, *Wilderness and the American Mind* (New Haven: Yale University Press, 1967), p. 116.

2. Philip Terrie, *Forever Wild: Environmental Aesthetics and the Adirondack Forest Preserve* (Philadelphia: Temple University Press, 1985).

3. Paul Jamieson, ed., *The Adirondack Reader* (Glens Falls, N.Y.: The Adirondack Mountain Club, 1982).

4. Elaine Showalter, "Feminist Criticism in the Wilderness," in *Writing and Sexual Difference*, ed. Elizabeth Abel, (Chicago: University of Chicago Press, 1980), p. 33.

5. Terrie, p. 45.

6. *Ibid.*, p. 12.

7. *Ibid.*, p. 43.

8. Showalter, pp. 16–17.

9. Marjorie Hope Nicolson, *Mountain Gloom and Mountain Glory: The Development of the Aesthetics of the Infinite* (Ithaca, NY: Cornell University Press, 1959), pp. 42–44.

10. Carol Gilligan, *In A Different Voice: Psychological Theory and Women's Development* (Cambridge: Harvard University Press, 1982), p. 100.

11. Gilligan, p. 127.

12. Elaine and William Hedges, *Land and Imagination: The Rural Dream in America* (Rochelle Park, N.J.: Hayden Book Co., 1980).

13. Jamieson, p. 99.

14. Jamieson, pp. 101–102.

15. *Ibid.*, p. 102.

16. Leonard Lutwack, *The Role of Place in Literature* (Syracuse, N.Y.: Syracuse University Press, 1984), p. 10.

202 NOTES

17. Susan Griffin, *Woman and Nature: The Roaring Inside Her* (New York: Harper and Row, 1978), p. xi.

Jeanne Robert Foster

1. Noel Riedinger-Johnson, ed. *Adirondack Portrait: A Piece of Time* (Syracuse, N.Y.: Syracuse University Press, 1986), p. 145.

2. Riedinger-Johnson, Personal papers. Schenectady, New York.

3. Riedinger-Johnson, *Adirondack Portraits*, p. xxi.

4. Riedinger-Johnson, Personal papers.

5. Richard Londraville, "The Many Careers of Jeanne Robert Foster," in *Biblion* (Winter 1968), p. 86.

6. Riedinger-Johnson, Personal papers, "Notes Presented at Poetry and Philosophy Group," 7 February 1963.

7. Jeanne Robert Foster, *Wild Apples* (Boston: Sherman, French and Co., 1916).

8. Richard Londraville, unpublished manuscript, biography of Jeanne Robert Foster, p. 40.

Lucia Newell Oliviere

1. Riedinger-Johnson, Personal papers.

Adelaide Crapsey

1. Susan Sutton Smith, *The Complete Poems and Collected Letters of Adelaide Crapsey* (Albany: State University of New York Press, 1977), p. 10.

2. Edward Butscher, *Adelaide Crapsey* (Boston: Twayne, 1979), p. 91.

3. Butscher, pp. 108–109.

4. Smith, p. 244.

5. *Ibid.*, p. 11.

6. *Ibid.*, p. 249.

Anne LaBastille

1. Anne LaBastille, "One Woman's Wilderness," *The Conservationist* (May--June 1985), p. 52.

2. Anne LaBastille, *Beyond Black Bear Lake* (New York: W.W. Norton & Co., 1987), p. 250.

3. Anne LaBastille, *Assignment: Wildlife* (New York: Dutton, 1980), p. 107.

4. Anne LaBastille, *Woodswoman* (New York: Dutton, 1976), p. 276.

5. LaBastille, *Black Bear Lake*, p. 222

6. LaBastille, *Ibid.*, p. 146.

7. LaBastille, *Woodswoman*, p. 239.

Martha Reben

1. Martha Reben, *The Healing Woods* (New York: Thomas Y. Crowell, 1952), p. 46.

2. *Ibid.*, p. 3.

3. *Ibid.*, p. 48.

4. *Ibid.*, p. 47.

5. *Ibid.*, p. 5.

6. Reben, *The Way of the Wilderness* (New York: Thomas Y. Crowell, 1955), p. 10.

7. *Ibid.*, p. 36.

8. *Ibid.*, p. 78.

9. *Ibid.*, p. 104.

10. *Ibid.*, p. 126.

11. *Ibid.*, p. 78.

12. *Ibid.*, p. 234.

Alice Gilborn

1. Alice Gilborn, *What Do You Do With A Kinkajou?* (New York: Lippincott, 1976), p. 36.

2. *Ibid.*, p. 36.

3. *Ibid.*, p. 38.

4. Alice Gilborn, *North Country* (Glens Falls, NY: Greenfield Review Press, 1986), p. 89.

5. Gilborn, *Kinkajou*, p. 112.

6. Alice Gilborn, "Landmarks," *Blueline* (Summer/Fall 1981), pp. 3–4.

7. Gilborn, *Kinkajou*, p. 57.

Jean Rikhoff

1. Jean Rikhoff, *One of the Raymonds* (New York: Dial Press, 1974), pp. 358–359.

2. Jean Rikhoff, *Buttes Landing* (New York: Dial Press, 1973), p. 3.

3. *Ibid.*, p. 10.

Bibliography

Introduction

Abel, Elizabeth, ed. *Writing and Sexual Difference*. Chicago: University of Chicago Press, 1982.

Galland, China. *Women in the Wilderness*. New York: Harper and Row, 1980.

Gilligan, Carol. *In A Different Voice: Psychological Theory and Women's Development*. Cambridge: Harvard University Press, 1982.

Goodfellow, Dorothy W., *Growing Up Wild*. Pacific Grove, CA: Boxwood Press, 1977.

Griffin, Susan. *Woman and Nature: The Roaring Inside Her*. New York: Harper and Row, 1978.

Hedges, Elaine nd William. *Land and Imagination: The Rural Dream in America*. Rochelle Park, NJ: Hayden Book Co., 1980.

Humphrey, William. *Ah! Wilderness! The Frontier in American Literature*. El Paso: University of El Paso, 1977.

Huth, Hans. *Nature and the American Mind: Three Centuries of Changing Attitudes*. Berkeley: University of California Press, 1957.

Jamieson, Paul, ed. *The Adirondack Reader*. Glens Falls, NY: The Adirondack Mountain Club, 1982.

Kolodny, Annette. *The Land Before Her: Fantasy and Experience of the American Frontiers, 1630–1860*. Chapel Hill: University of North Carolina Press, 1984.

——. *The Lay of the Land: Metaphor as Experience and History in American Life and Letters*. Chapel Hill: University of North Carolina Press, 1975.

Lutwack, Leonard. *The Role of Place in Literature*. Syracuse, NY: Syracuse University Press, 1984.

Nash, Roderick. *Wilderness and the American Mind*. New Haven: Yale University Press, 1967.

Nicolson, Marjorie Hope. *Mountain Gloom and Mountain Glory: The Development of the Aesthetics of the Infinite*. Ithaca, NY: Cornell University Press, 1959.

206

BIBLIOGRAPHY

Taylor, Robert. *Saranac: America's Magic Mountain*. Boston: Houghton Mifflin, 1986.

Terrie, Philip G. *Forever Wild: Environmental Aesthetics and the Adirondack Forest Preserve*. Philadelphia: Temple University Press, 1985.

Diaries of May Dell Cheney, Mrs. H. M. Clark, Juliet Baker Kellogg, Rosannah M. Wheelock, and Helen Wardwell, Adirondack Museum Library, Blue Mountain Lake, New York.

Jeanne Robert Foster

Foster, Jeanne Robert. *Neighbors of Yesterday*. Boston: Sherman, French and Co., 1916.

———. *Wild Apples*. Boston: Sherman, French and Co., 1916 (Julie Ollivier).

———. *Rock Flower*. NY: Boni and Liveright, 1923. (Mrs. Jeanne Robert Oliver Foster)

———. *Marthe*. Boston: Sherman, French and Co., (Noel Armstrong) 1927.

———. *Awakening Grace*. North Myrtle Beach, S.C.: Sherlar Press, 1977.

Gilborn, Alice. "Jeanne Foster: A Woman of Parts." *Blueline* (Winter/Spring 1984): 1–4.

———. "Jeanne Foster: The Poetry of Place." *Blueline* (Summer/Fall 1984): 1–5.

Londraville, Richard. "The Many Careers of Jeanne Robert Foster." *Biblion* (Winter 1968): vol. 1, no. 2, pp. 84–87.

———. Unpublished manuscript, biography of Jeanne Robert Foster.

Riedinger-Johnson, Noel, ed. *Adirondack Portraits: A Piece of Time*. Syracuse, NY: Syracuse University Press, 1986.

Foster-Murphy and Quinn-Foster-Yeats Collections, Rare Books and Manuscripts. New York Public Library, New York, New York.
Noel Riedinger-Johnson. Personal papers. Schenectady, New York.

Lucia N. Oliviere

Foster, Jeanne Robert. *Adirondack Portraits: A Piece of Time*. Noel Riedinger-Johnson, ed. Syracuse, NY: Syracuse University Press, 1986.

Oliviere, Lucia N. *Old Houses*. New York: Oscar A. Randel, 1928.

"Lucia N. Oliviere," *The Citizen* (July 1, 1927: p. 1.

The John Thurman Historical Society Quarterly (March 1967), pp. 1–2.

Riedinger-Johnson, Noel. Personal papers. Schenectady, New York.

Adelaide Crapsey

Butscher, Edward. *Adelaide Crapsey*. Boston: Twayne U.S. Author Series, 1979.

Osborn, Mary Elizabeth. *Adelaide Crapsey*. Boston: Bruce Humphries, 1933.

Smith, Susan Sutton. *The Complete Poems and Collected Letters of Adelaide Crapsey*. Albany: State University of New York Press, 1977.

Taylor, Robert. *Saranac: America's Magic Mountain*. Boston: Houghton Mifflin, 1986.

Anne LaBastille

Anne LaBastille, *Woodswoman*. New York: Dutton, 1976.

——. *Assignment: Wildlife*. New York: Dutton, 1980.

——. *Women and Wilderness*. San Francisco: Sierra Club Books, 1980.

——. *Beyond Black Bear Lake*. New York: W.W. Norton & Co., 1987.

——. "My Backyard, The Adirondacks. *National Geographic* (May 1975), 147: 616–639.

——. "One Woman's Wilderness." *The Conservationist* (May–June 1985), 39: 50–53.

Martha Reben

Reben, Martha. *The Healing Woods*. New York: Thomas Y. Crowell, 1952.

——. *The Way of the Wilderness*. New York: Thomas Y. Crowell, 1955. Manuscript, Saranac Lake Free Library, Saranac Lake, New York.

——. *A Sharing of Joy*. New York: Harcourt, Brace and World, 1963.

Rice, Fred. "Fifty Years in a Health Resort." Albany: J. B. Lyon Company, 1937.

Roseberry, Charles R. "Martha Reben: Wilderness Lady." *Adirondack Life* (Summer 1975), vol. 6. pp. 50 ff.

Alice Wolf Gilborn

Gilborn, Alice Wolf. *What Do You Do With A Kinkajou?* New York: Lippincott, 1976.

——. "Portents" and "Evening and Early Sorrow." *North Country*. Glen Falls, N.Y.: Greenfield Review Press, 1986.

——. "Birds." *The Writer* (July 1979), 92:18.

——. "When the Ice Goes Out." *Blueline* (Summer/Fall 1979), I:28.

——. "Of Birth and Blueline." *Blueline* (Winter/Spring 1981), 2:4–6.

——. "Landmarks." *Blueline* (Summer/Fall 1981), 3:3–4.

——. "Living With the Animals." *Blueline* (Summer/Fall 1982), 4:1–4.

——. "Out of the Blue." *Blueline* (Summer/Fall 1983), 5:1–3.

——. "Alien Woods." *Adirondack Empire* (1984), I:28.

——. "The Proving Grounds." *Blueline* (Winter/Spring 1986), 7:1–2.

Jean Rikhoff

Rikhoff, Jean. *Buttes Landing*. New York: Dial Press, 1973.

——. *One of the Raymonds*. New York: Dial Press, 1974.

——. *The Sweetwater*. New York: Dial Press, 1976.

——. "Grieving the Garden of Eden." *Esprit*, vol. II, no. 1 (Fall 1985), p. 98.

Printed in the United States
56223LVS00004B/208-216